W9-CJM-286

A Guide to Archival Sources for Italian-American Art History in the Archives of American Art

ARCHIVES OF AMERICAN ART

SMITHSONIAN INSTITUTION

Reference
BOSTON
PUBLIC
LIBRARY

A GUIDE TO ARCHIVAL SOURCES FOR ITALIAN-AMERICAN ART HISTORY IN THE ARCHIVES OF AMERICAN ART

Archives of American Art

American Art-Portrait Gallery Building
Smithsonian Institution
8th & G Streets, N.W.
Washington, D.C. 20560

THE ARCHIVES OF AMERICAN ART, founded in 1954, has assembled the world's largest collection of records documenting the history of the visual arts in the United States. More than 10 million items of original source material are available for study to scholars, students, writers, and other researchers. A bureau of the Smithsonian Institution since 1970, the Archives preserves its original documents in Washington, D.C. The most actively used collections are microfilmed and microfilm copies are deposited at the Archives' centers in Washington, New York, Boston, Detroit, San Francisco and San Marino, California. The original material is thus protected from loss or destruction while copies are readily accessible to scholars in the centers or through inter-library loan. The Archives has not only the records of American painters, sculptors, craftsmen, collectors, and dealers, but also those of critics, historians, curators, museums, societies, and other institutions concerned with art in America.

Affiliation with the Smithsonian Institution makes the Archives of American Art part of one of the world's greatest research centers in the arts and sciences. However, the Institution's support does not cover all of the Archives' operating costs. The Archives' Trustees raise a substantial portion of the annual budget through private gifts. Such funding underwrites approximately half of the staff, supports national collecting, and enables the Archives to publish its quarterly "Journal" and other contributions to scholarship.

OFFICES OF THE ARCHIVES OF AMERICAN ART SMITHSONIAN INSTITUTION

8th and G Streets, NW, Washington, DC 20560 (202) 357-2781
1285 Avenue of the Americas, New York, NY 10019 (212) 399-5015
5200 Woodward Avenue, Detroit, MI 48202 (313) 226-7544
87 Mount Vernon Street, Boston, MA 02108 (617) 565-8444
Huntington Library, 1151 Oxford Road, San Marino, CA 91108 (818) 405-7847

INTER-LIBRARY LOAN OF MICROFILMS

All Archives microfilm that has not been restricted can be borrowed through regular interlibrary loan procedures, eight rolls at a time, for a period of one month, renewable depending on demand. Address all loan requests to the Detroit office of the Archives at the above address.

Library of Congress Catalog Card Number: 92-082761
ISBN Number: 1-880193-03-5

TRUSTEES AND STAFF

Contents

Acknowledgments

This work was prepared almost entirely by interns and volunteers. We can hardly exaggerate the debt we owe these enthusiastic, unpaid individuals and we thank them sincerely. They include Anna Athanasopoulou, Wendy Bellion, Heather Campbell, Kelly Gray, Danielle Katz, Jill Lundin, Susan Spaulding, Sarah Vowell, and Deborah White. We hope that their experience here and the knowledge that their work has resulted in this publication will have made it worthwhile.

We wish to thank the Henry Luce Foundation, Inc., for its generous support of the Archives' national collecting programs. The funds provided by the Foundation have not only helped to underwrite the search for original documentary materials in areas of the country in which the Archives has not been able to work previously, but has enabled the publication of finding aids and guides such as this one on Italian-American resources at the Archives, thus providing researchers with easier access to our collections.

Richard J. Wattenmaker
Director

Foreword

Who, what, where, when, why? Ask a question about American artists, patrons, and institutions touching on Italy and the chances are excellent that you will be led to the needed information through this *Guide to Archival Sources for Italian-American Art History in the Archives of American Art.* A handy tool, but much more than that, the *Guide* is a sophisticated instrument that will be indispensable to any researcher concerned with Italian-American cultural and artistic connections from the early nineteenth century to about 1980.

The entries in the *Guide* are exemplary, providing excellent descriptions of the content of each archival unit, most of which are headed by the name of an individual, with his or her birth and death dates, nationality and profession (American painter, sculptor, art critic, etc.) and location(s) of the writer at the time of writing the document (Alan Robert Solomon [1920-1973] American art critic and historian, U.S. commissioner of the Biennale, Venice, Italy). A few entries deal with institutions including the Pennsylvania Academy of the Fine Arts, the American Academy in Rome, and the Italy America Society, among others. The microfilm roll and frame number are given for each entry, together with the actual location of the documents. Because the entries are so specific, the *Guide* can be used as a time-saver for the researcher who knows exactly what he or she is looking for; because the volume is a compendium of the Archives' vast microfilm library and its own holdings of original documents plus those of other institutions, it can serve as a suggestive field to explore for new insights.

One can simply read the volume for its intrinsic interest. Leafing through the pages, one's eye catches intriguing references to almost every facet of the work and experiences of American artists in Italy. Many documents detail their everyday life, and it is fascinating to notice who were the American artists, patrons, dealers, and literary figures in Italy in the mid-nineteenth century, say, and to discover their relations with one another: Thomas Buchanan Read, for example, was a poet as well as painter and numbered among his acquaintances and correspondents Nathaniel Hawthorne and Henry Wadsworth Longfellow, to whose letters one is led in the *Guide*; William Page's letters from his patrons and friends, Robert and Elizabeth Browning, are signaled in the entry for Page. One notes how insular the American group was; there was apparently very little contact with Italian artists, and the *Guide* triggers the question of the language barrier--did some of the Americans learn, or try to acquire, some knowledge of Italian?

The *Guide* points to interesting insights into American political attitudes regarding events in Italy such as the comment in a letter of James Freeman that deals with the siege of Rome by French troops in 1849. In fact, American reactions to the people, the landscape, the religion, as well as politics--every aspect of Italian culture, it seems--can be discovered through the *Guide*'s description of the letters, the diaries, the sketchbooks, the catalogs on microfilm or in collections. The material has been in the Archives, of course; the difficulty was always to get at the information one needed.

Finally it may be said that among the blessings of this *Guide* is its index, which gives the page number of the main entry plus those of other entries where that name appears.

What a boon this publication is will be appreciated first and foremost by American art historians who did not have it at their disposal; let younger scholars make the most of it!

Irma B. Jaffe
Professor (emeritus) of Art History,
Fordham University
Cultural Consultant, the Italian

Introduction

The Archives of American Art was founded in 1954 to locate, preserve, and microfilm papers documenting the history of art in America. In 1970 it became a bureau of the Smithsonian Institution in Washington and now operates out of that city and from offices in New York City, Boston, Detroit, and San Marino, where copies of Archives' microfilms are available for research use.

This guide is one of a series of publications designed to bring to light the rich resources of the Archives of American Art, in this case the many letters, diaries, and other papers that provide insight into the relationship between the Italian and American art worlds. It is not a guide to collections but to those parts of collections (sometimes only a few letters out of hundreds) that concern this topic.

Entries are placed chronologically by the earliest year of the papers, an arrangement that tends to group papers of a certain era. However, as some collections span 50 years or more, grouping by era is only approximate. There is an alphabetical index of personal names, place names, and names of organizations.

The original papers are in the Archives of American Art unless otherwise noted. Collections that have been microfilmed have an identifying roll number at the end of the entry. Microfilms are available at each office of the Archives and worldwide through interlibrary loan. Up-to-date information about the Archives' collections is available on the international database of the Research Libraries Information Network (RLIN), now in many libraries.

Arthur J. Breton
Senior Archivist

PENNSYLVANIA ACADEMY OF THE FINE ARTS
Philadelphia, Pa.

Letter from Pietro Ancora to the directors, outlining a plan for an academy of Roman art to be associated with the Pennsylvania Academy, July 8, 1807. Ancora presents fund-raising ideas, includes cost estimates, and offers to go to Rome to purchase molds, paintings, and casts of statues and busts for American students to study. Microfilm roll P 63, frames 181-183. Original in the Pennsylvania Academy of the Fine Arts, Philadelphia, Pa.

Two letters from James Abercrombie to the directors regarding [Enrico] Causici, an Italian sculptor working in the United States, December 7, 1816, and January 7, 1817. Abercrombie requests that the Academy provide studio space for Causici to sculpt an equestrian statue of George Washington to be installed in the Academy. He asks if he can borrow Causici's earlier bust of George Washington to use as a model. Microfilm roll P 63, frames 414-419. Originals in the Pennsylvania Academy of the Fine Arts, Philadelphia, Pa.

Letter from Anthony Morris to Joseph Hopkinson, president of the Academy, February 16, 1817. Morris suggests that the Academy hire a representative in Italy to arrange for the shipping of paintings to Philadelphia and to provide information about the best art schools, current artistic trends, and most prominent artists. Morris highly recommends Gilbert Stuart Newton of Boston, Mass., for this position. Microfilm roll P 63, frames 421-423. Original in the Pennsylvania Academy of the Fine Arts, Philadelphia, Pa.

Acquisition record documenting the receipt by the Academy of Paolo Veronese's *Saint John the Baptist* (16 x 20 in.), presented by Mr. and Mrs. John W. Field in 1887. Microfilm roll P 80, frame 632. Original in the Pennsylvania Academy of the Fine Arts, Philadelphia, Pa.

Acquisition record documenting the receipt by the Academy of a painting by Bonifazio Veronese titled *The Last Supper* (38 x 18 in.), presented by Mr. and Mrs. John W. Field in 1887. Also included is a brief biography of the artist. Microfilm roll P 80, frames 630-631. Original in the Pennsylvania Academy of the Fine Arts, Philadelphia, Pa.

Material relating to the Academy's acquisitions of Hiram Powers's marble bust *Proserpine* and plaster cast *California* (8 items). Included are 1 photograph of *Proserpine*, 1939; registration and biographical data; 3 letters, 1940, regarding the lending of *Proserpine*; and a 1945 essay titled "Powers' *Proserpine*" about how the bust was commissioned by Edward Carey, the former president of the Academy (3 pp.). Microfilm roll P 78. Originals in the Pennsylvania Academy of the Fine Arts, Philadelphia, Pa.

Two letters and 1 photograph, 1947, relating to William Henry Rinehart's sculpture *Hero*, completed in Rome in 1855. Microfilm roll P 78, frames 272-276. Originals in the Pennsylvania Academy of the Fine Arts, Philadelphia, Pa.

BENJAMIN WEST (1738-1820)
American painter, London, England

Letter from the officers of the Academy [of St. Luke] in Rome asking West to accept an honorary membership, January 23, 1816. Microfilm roll P 24, frame 537. Original in the Historical Society of Pennsylvania, Philadelphia, Pa.

HORATIO GREENOUGH (1805-1852)
Sculptor, Florence, Italy

Letter to Robert Gilmor of Baltimore, Md., May 16, 1822. Greenough says he has completed a sculpture group model for J[ames] F[enimore] Cooper that Cooper has offered to exhibit, and that the bust he is making for Gilmor should arrive in New York in August. Microfilm roll P 21, frame 57. Original in the Historical Society of Pennsylvania, Philadelphia, Pa.

Letters (1 to each): Robert Gilmor says he will be able to continue his work in Italy thanks to Greenough and others, May 17, 1828; to Major Poussin introducing Emilio Santarelli, March 30, 1837; to Henry K[irke] Brown introducing John Cadman, January 1, 1845; and to R[ichard] H[enry] Wilde about a marriage, undated. Microfilm roll P 22, frames 186-189. Originals in the Historical Society of Pennsylvania, Philadelphia, Pa.

Letters from friends, acquaintances, and U.S. government officials received while he was living in Florence, 1829-1852 (74 items). Included are ca. 15 letters from James Fenimore Cooper expressing confidence in Greenough's ability as a sculptor, describing activities of other artists, mentioning an upcoming commission for a statue of George Washington, and advising that it would be best for Greenough's career for him to remain in Italy rather than go to England. A contract from President Martin Van Buren outlines compositional requirements, completion time, and schedule of payments to Greenough for a sculpture for the steps of the U.S. Capitol. Included are ca. 20 letters from Edward Everett commenting on Greenough's progress on sculptures, including *Washington*. Others write of the artistic activity in Florence and seek advice about antique sculptures. Microfilm roll 1215, frames 358-601. Originals privately owned.

Letter, addressed "Dear Madam," containing a bill for the chimney pieces he made, October 3, 1837. Greenough apologizes for the delay caused by import restrictions. Microfilm roll D 5, frame 119. Original in the Detroit Institute of Arts, Detroit, Mich.

ANTONIO CANOVA (1757-1822)
Italian sculptor, Rome, Italy

Letter in Italian, with an English translation, to John Trumbull in England concerning Canova's commission to make a sculpture in memory of [George] Washington, June 6,

1822 (4 pp.). Canova discusses the problem of casting the sculpture. Microfilm roll N 68-12, frames 3-4. Original in the Pierpont Morgan Library, New York, N.Y.

ROBERT WALTER WEIR (1803-1889)
American painter, Rome and Florence, Italy

Correspondence relating to his travel and study in Rome and Florence, 1824-1826 (8 letters). Included are 4 letters from Horatio Greenough, Weir's roommate in Rome, written from Florence, Paris, and Marseille, in which Greenough discusses his new home in Florence, mutual friends, and fellow artists. Also included are 4 letters from Weir to New York City Mayor John Ferguson, his future father-in-law, describing his experiences in Italy and noting, "I am at present making studies for an original picture--the subject is the making of a nun, at which ceremony I was present." Microfilm roll 531.

Sketchbook kept by Weir while studying in Rome, 1826 (111 pp.). Using pencil, ink wash, and pen and ink, Weir depicts figure studies, groups of nuns, religious scenes, and architectural features (see above, April 25, 1826). Microfilm roll 726.

SAMUEL FINLEY BREESE MORSE (1791-1872)
Painter, inventor, New York, N.Y.

Letter to Simeon De Witt Bloodgood, Albany, N.Y., December 29, 1833. After reporting that Piero Maroncelli will write about the political climate in Italy for Bloodgood's newspaper, Morse expresses frustration at not being able to reach his artistic goals. Microfilm roll P 22, frame 328. Original in the Historical Society of Pennsylvania, Philadelphia, Pa.

Letter to Horatio Greenough introducing Thomas Prichard Rossiter, 1840. Morse writes that Rossiter will make a study tour of England, France, and Italy. He recommends Rossiter highly and asks Greenough to assist him in any way possible. Also included is a photograph of a portrait of Morse painted by Edward Lind Morse. Microfilm roll D 33, frame 425.

HIRAM POWERS (1805-1873)
American sculptor, Florence, Italy

Correspondence with his benefactors, John S. Preston and family, in South Carolina and Europe, 1836-1876 (56 items). Powers discusses his progress on the busts of John C. Calhoun, Henry Clay, and Daniel Webster; the delays in government funding for commissions; his political views; and his family. Preston indicates his family's pleasure with the busts Powers completed for them and with the widespread respect that Powers has acquired in Europe and the United States. Also included is a typescript pertaining to the purchase of Raphael's *The Madonna of the Window*, which Powers had bought in Rome for the Preston family. Microfilm roll 74, frames 154-289.

Papers, mostly correspondence with his patrons, friends, family, and business associates, 1837-1873 (18,200 items). Frequent correspondents include Sam Y. Atlee, Sidney Brooks, Thomas Crawford, Charles M. Eaton, Edward Everett, M.M. Holloway, Miner K. Kellogg, Nicholas Longworth, Sir John Naesmyth, and Dr. James Playfair. Also included are stories, essays, notes, poems, and commentaries by Powers and others; patents, agreements, contracts, and descriptions of his inventories; financial material, including accounts with Sidney Brooks, Miner K. Kellogg, and other patrons; an autograph album containing handwritten poems by Robert and Elizabeth Browning, William Cullen Bryant, Bayard Taylor, and others; data on Powers's sculpture, including prices; newspaper clippings; and an exhibition catalog (microfilm roll 1147). An inventory of the correspondence is included on microfilm roll 1131. Microfilm rolls 1131-1147.

Photographs of Powers; his family; his studio; Florentine landscapes; pieces by him and others; Carrara marble quarries; numerous English artists; and famous personalities, including, Thomas Ball, Sarah Bernhardt, Edwin Booth, Prof. [Giovanni] Dupré, Charles F. Fuller, Joel T. Hart, Jenny Lind, L[arkin] G. Mead, and John Ruskin. Also included is an album of photographs of Florentine sculpture and buildings and of sculpture by Canova, Longworth, Powers, Preston, and others. Microfilm roll 1147, frames 201-896.

Two letters to Bayard Taylor, October 9, 1845, and February 2, 1846. Powers writes about lending money to Taylor and expresses delight with Taylor's poem inspired by Powers's sculpture *Eve*. Microfilm roll N 68-10. Originals in the Pierpont Morgan Library, New York, N.Y.

Typescript of Paul B. Metzler's master's thesis for Ohio State University, "The Sculpture of Hiram Powers" (1939, 240 pp.). Prepared as a *catalogue raisonné*, it includes appendices, illustrations, letters, a chronology, and bibliography. Microfilm roll D 23, frames 594-904.

Typescript by Clara Louise Dentler, titled "White Marble--The Life and Letters of Hiram Powers" (ca. 1940s?, 322 pp.). It includes notes, appendix, illustrations, and a copy of Powers's genealogical chart. Microfilm roll 1102, frames 1385-1580, and roll 1103, frames 1-131.

HENRY INMAN (1801-1846)
Painter, New York, N.Y.

Letter to Philip Hone introducing Signor F. Celestine of Florence as the proprietor of the pictures being exhibited at Clinton Hall, October 12, 1837. Inman mentions that Celestine has a plan for New York City to acquire some of these pictures. Microfilm roll D 294, frame 737.

CHAUNCY BRADLEY IVES (1810-1894)
American sculptor, Rome, Italy

Six letters to Ives and his wife from friends in the United States, 1838-1883. Correspondents include C[harles] W. Chauncy, C.D. Roberts, H[arriet] Beecher Stowe, and C[aroline] Tilton. Microfilm roll 3134, frames 606-626.

GEORGE LORING BROWN (1814-1889)
American painter, Boston, Mass. and Rome and Florence, Italy

Diary kept by Brown's wife, Harriet, on her trip to Rome, 1840-1841 (66 pp.). The diary begins aboard ship, August 16, 1840. The narrative is often directed to her brother and sisters. She describes her intense feelings of homesickness; her impressions of Rome's inhabitants, street life, and surrounding countryside; the malaria epidemics during the summers; and the death and funeral parade of Princess Borghese. Mrs. Brown mentions Thomas Crawford and the American consul, Mr. [George W.] Greene, and discusses the commissions her husband has received from Americans traveling in Rome. She writes of her hopes to persuade him to copy a picture of a young girl in the Borghese Palace. Also included is a sketchbook by George Loring Brown with notations in the margins referring to places in Italy (undated, 24 pp.). Microfilm roll 498.

Typescript of Thomas Whittlesey Leavitt's doctoral dissertation for Harvard University, "The Life, Work, and Significance of George Loring Brown" (1957, 226 pp.). Included is a chapter about his expatriate years in Rome and Florence, 1840-1859, and a bibliography, appendices, and illustrations of Brown's works. Microfilm roll D 169, frames 19-257.

FRANCIS WILLIAM EDMONDS (1806-1863)
American art patron, painter, Italy

Diary kept while traveling through England, France, and Italy, November 25, 1840-July 29, 1841 (232 pp.). Edmonds describes Roman ruins, sight-seeing, his day-to-day activities, impressions of the Italian countryside, and his frequent visits to the Villa Borghese to see the paintings and on one occasion to copy them. He writes about searching in Italian "picture shops" for paintings to send back to the United States and the restrictions that the Italian government had placed on exporting works of art. Throughout the diary he refers to his sketching and painting, and he offers an eyewitness account of the Carnival and the Holy Week in Rome. Edmonds refers to [John William] Casilear, [Francis Marion] Crawford, [Asher B.] Durand, and [Luther] Terry. Durand accompanied him on most of his trip through Italy, and they often visited the studios of [Vincenzo] Cammucini, [Horatio] Greenough, Podesti, [Hiram] Powers, and Thorwaldsen. Included is a list of Americans in Rome in July 1841 (frame 98); an itemized list of his expenditures, including food, hotels, servants, and transportation costs (4 pp., frames 89, 97, and 100); and a list of the objects and places to see in each city (3 pp., frames 92-93). Microfilm roll 1285, frames 14-180.

MINER KILBOURNE KELLOGG (1814-1889)
American painter, New York, N.Y., Rome, Italy, and Paris, France

Papers, including correspondence dealing mainly with his promotion of Hiram Powers's *Greek Slave* (ca. 100 items). Included are letters from the following dignitaries, patrons, and artists to Kellogg in Florence, 1841-1852: Park Benjamin, Edward Everett, Reverdy Johnson, Edward Kavanagh, Major Philip Kearny, Caroline M. Kirkland, William C. Macready, George Perkins Marsh, Joel R. Poinsett, Bayard Taylor, Osmond Tiffany, Henry Theodore Tuckerman, and R. Wickliffe, Jr. In addition, 6 letters from American sculptress Vinnie Ream (later Hoxie) in Florence ask for Kellogg's assistance with her work, 1868-1869. Microfilm roll D 30, frames 41-348, and roll D 33, frames 427-451.

Scrapbook of newspaper clippings collected by him from American and Italian newspapers, 1842-1882. Included are 4 reproductions of Kellogg's letters to his brother, A.H. Layard, and to Robert Wickliffe, Jr., 1844-1847, describing his travels and Layard's archeological discoveries; Kellogg's description of his Florence studio, titled "Devils in an Artist's Studio"; 6 promotions, in English and Italian, of Kellogg and his work in Italy; and a pamphlet, *Mr. Miner K. Kellogg to His Friends* (Paris, 1858, 24 pp.), in which Kellogg describes the reasons for his estrangement from Hiram Powers. Microfilm roll 986, frames 1076-1192.

Correspondence and documents relating to *Herodias*, a painting owned by Kellogg and believed by him to be an original Leonardo da Vinci, 1857-1876 and 1945. Included is Kellogg's pamphlet titled *Documents Relating to a Picture by Leonardo da Vinci, Entitled Herodias* (1868, 36 pp.), and a typed list of Old Master Italian paintings in Kellogg's collection. Microfilm roll D 30, frames 921-972.

THOMAS COLE (1801-1848)
Painter, Catskill, N.Y.

Letter to George W. Greene, American consul in Rome, August 29, 1842. Cole writes that he has visited friends since his return from Italy but has not painted. He explains that he has heard about [Hiram] Powers's great popularity but does not think the attention entirely deserved. Cole also reports that [Thomas Prichard] Rossiter has had trouble over the rent for his studio in Rome. He says [Samuel F.B.] Morse is working on the telegraph and reports that Morse will receive a surprising $700 a year to work on administrative details for the American Academy [of Arts and Letters]. Microfilm roll D 8, frames 482-485.

HENRY KIRKE BROWN (1814-1886)
American sculptor, Florence and Rome, Italy

Letters from Brown and his wife, Lydia, to friends and family in the United States, December 1842-November 1845 (ca. 28 items). Brown writes about the statues on which he is working and reports that he works up to 10-12 hours a day. He also writes of financial and domestic matters, his mixed feelings about the Catholic church, and [Hiram] Powers's work. Lydia writes that she is learning Italian, frequently asks for news from home, and notes that the newspaper in Woodstock, Vt., reported incorrectly that jealous Italian sculptors were plotting to assassinate [Hiram] Powers. Microfilm roll 2770, frames not numbered.

Letter to E.P. Prentice in Albany, N.Y., October 2, 1843. Brown writes that he is going to Rome for the winter because he has heard there are more commissions there. He says that he hopes to find a buyer for his statue in Rome and that some have said it is the best work ever completed by an American. Microfilm roll P 22, frame 75.

Letter from Seth Wells Cheney, Manchester, Conn., to Brown in Rome, December 1, 1844. Cheney describes his travels to Genoa, Florence, and Naples. Microfilm roll P 22, frame 101.

E[DWARD] L. CAREY (d. 1845)
Bookseller, collector, Philadelphia, Pa.

Two letters from Hiram Powers in Florence, January 1, 1843, and March 27, 1845. Powers writes of the quality of different marbles and notes that he uses Carrara marble in all his works. He informs Carey that he will start work on the bust and the vase. In the 1845 letter, he informs Carey that the bust is finally finished and ready to be sent to the United States and reports that he is now working on a pedestal for the bust, to be sent at a later date. Microfilm roll P 22, frames 391-392. Originals in the Historical Society of Pennsylvania, Philadelphia, Pa.

THOMAS CRAWFORD (1813-1857)
American sculptor, Rome, Italy

Letters to his wife, Louisa, from Rome, 1845-1857 (49 items). Crawford discusses everyday life, family matters, and financial concerns. He writes that he is working on a statue of Beethoven and mentions other American artists in Italy, including [John Gadsby] Chapman, [Horatio] Greenough, and Hiram Powers. Crawford says he dislikes Harriet Hosmer and [Joseph] Mozier. Microfilm roll D 181, frames 636-946. Typescripts on microfilm roll 3023, frames 710-1035. Typescripts privately owned.

HENRY GREENOUGH (1807-1883)
FRANCES BOOTT GREENOUGH (1809-1897)
Americans in Italy

Letters to their families and friends in Massachusetts, 1845-1891 (ca. 100 items). The letters describe everyday life as expatriate Americans in Florence as well as frequent travels through Italy and in Austria, Germany, and Malta accompanied at times by Henry's brother, Horatio Greenough. Included are 6 drawings by Henry Greenough and ca. 10 letters, primarily about family matters, that Henry and Frances wrote to each other while Henry traveled without his family. Microfilm roll 1215, frames 1-357. Originals privately owned.

FRANK DUVENECK (1848-1919)
ELIZABETH BOOTT DUVENECK (d. 1888)
Painter and teacher, Florence and Venice, Italy

Correspondence of Frank and Elizabeth Boott Duveneck, 1845-1919. Included are 2 letters from Duveneck to [Theodore] Wores, 1 letter to Duveneck from his wife, 7 letters to her friend Bessie Girling, and a 50-pp. account of Elizabeth Duveneck's travels in Europe, sent to her father. Elizabeth Duveneck writes 11 letters from France, Rome, and Venice to William Morris Hunt's painting class describing her travels and study with Duveneck in Munich and Venice. William Copley writes from Florence requesting payment for marble and labor, December 6, 1893, and February 25, 1895. Also included are 7 letters from Julius Rolshoven describing his work, his exhibitions, family matters, and outings in London with [Charles Dana?] Gibson, Henschel, Henry James, [Francis Davis?] Millet, and John Singer Sargent. Microfilm roll 1097.

Correspondence, sketchbooks, and journals relating to Frank and Elizabeth Boott Duveneck's work and travel in Italy, 1855-1893. After studying in Venice together with John Henry Twachtman and William Merritt Chase in 1877, Duveneck moved his art school from Munich to Italy. He spent his summers in Venice and his winters in Florence with his students, who were collectively known as the "Duveneck Boys" and included John Alexander, Otto Henry Bacher, his future wife Elizabeth Boott, Joseph de Camp, Julius Rolshoven, Henry Rosenberg, Twachtman, Theodore Wendel, and Theodore Wores. Duveneck left Italy following the death of his wife in 1888. Correspondence includes 5 letters from Elizabeth Boott in Florence to her uncle, Arthur Lyman, describing her childhood activities, 1856-1857; 3 letters to an unnamed friend regarding her new husband and married life, 1886-1887; and 5 letters to her father relating family news and asking him to contact [William Merritt?] Chase in Boston, 1887. Included is 1 letter to Duveneck's former student Wores, March 29, 1915; and 1 letter from Duveneck to his brother Charles, regarding the death of Elizabeth, March 28, 1888. Sculptor William Couper writes from Florence about details of the sale and the blocking of marble for Duveneck's memorial statue to his wife, 1893, and Daniel Chester French writes to Duveneck's son, proposing a bronze cast of the same statue, April 24, 1926. Also included are letters to Duveneck's son and daughter-in-law from Adelaide B. Wadsworth and Charles Mills, describing their experiences as students of Duveneck in Boston and Italy. Microfilm roll 1150.

Seven sketchbooks, including one kept by Elizabeth Boott in Italy, which contains portraits of American expatriates in Italy, including Robert Browning, Chauncy Ives, Elihu Vedder, and Boott's father, 1855. An undated sketchbook belonging to Duveneck includes drawings of Venetian canals, architecture, and street scenes. Two unsigned sketchbooks labeled "Bagni di Caseiana, August 1885," and "The Grandfather," feature landscape and figure studies. Also included is "The Legend of Monteripdo," a fairy tale by Boott set in Italy; and a handwritten, illustrated notebook titled "Academy Notes, Duveneck School, December 25, 1880 . . . edited and arranged by J. Rushing," which is a wry critique of works by contemporaneous artists and the "Duveneck Boys." Miscellaneous items include catalogs, clippings, and other printed material. Microfilm rolls 1150-1151.

Eighty-four head and caricature pencil sketches by Frank Duveneck of the "Duveneck Boys." Although the sketches are not labeled or dated, one includes the notation "Nov. 1879," suggesting that the sketches were created in Venice. Two sketches resemble James McNeill Whistler, who was studying with the Duveneck circle in Venice in 1879. Microfilm roll 792.

E[MANUEL GOTTLIEB] LEUTZE (1816-1868)
American painter, Rome, Italy

Two letters, April 25, 1845, and undated. In the 1845 letter to W. Norris in Vienna, he writes that he has received a draft on Norris from E[dward] L. Carey of Philadelphia and has deposited it. In the letter to P[eter] Vroom, Berlin, Leutze writes that he has located a print of his *Washington*, which he will send to Vroom. Microfilm roll P 20, frames 513-514. Originals in the Historical Society of Pennsylvania, Philadelphia, Pa.

JOHN F. KENSETT (1816-1872)
American painter, Italy

Journal written while in London, while traveling from Rome to Naples, and during his passage to the United States from England, 1847 (15 pp.). Kensett describes the experience of traveling yet says very little about cities visited. He writes of his voyage from Rome to Naples on board the *Maria Antoinette* and describes arriving in the bay of Naples at sunrise. Microfilm roll N 738, frames 587-599. Original privately owned.

GEORGE HENRY YEWELL (1830-1923)
American painter, Italy

Diary, kept sporadically between 1847 and 1875, including an account of a trip to Italy in 1867 with Henry Augustus Loop and their wives (288 pp.). Yewell describes their leisurely trip to Venice, where he and Loop toured the city, visited the Bayard Taylors, and copied, painted, and sketched works. During a winter in Rome, Yewell writes about his painting, the sights of Rome, Christmas and Easter services at St. Peter's, finding an apartment and a studio, and Roman social life, including activities with Charles Coleman, Charlotte Cushman, Thomas Hotchkiss, William [Morris] Hunt, Robert Macpherson, Thomas Buchanan Read, Charles Stanley Reinhart, Bayard Taylor, and Elihu Vedder. The remainder of the diary was kept at various times in Italy, beginning June 11, 1869, with an account of painting in Venice with Sanford Gifford. Yewell writes about a trip to Chioggia, working at San Marco, painting commissions for Americans, the difficulties of painting in bad weather, and the excitement in Venice caused by military events on September 6, 1870. In addition, he mentions staying at Loop's home and a visit in Perugia with a Mr. Connolly and [Truman H.?] Bartlett. Microfilm roll 2428. Originals in the University of Iowa, Iowa City, Iowa.

Autographs of visitors to studio receptions in Rome, 1874-1874 (29 pp.). Microfilm roll 2428, frames 38-65. Originals in the University of Iowa, Iowa City, Iowa.

JASPER CROPSEY (1823-1900)
American landscape painter, Italy

Sketchbook kept in Italy, 1848-1849 (ca. 74 pp.). Cropsey depicts landscapes, trees, buildings, and animals and includes occasional pages of writings. Microfilm roll 4086, frames not numbered.

Six letters to him in Rome, 1848-1849. Included are 4 letters from John M. Falconer; 1 from sculptor William Wetmore Story, expressing regrets that they could not meet; and 1 from the banking house Maquay Hooker, informing Cropsey that letters are being forwarded to him in Lucca. Microfilm roll 337.

JAMES FREEMAN (1808-1884)
American painter, Rome, Italy

Four letters to collector W.D. Pickman, Salem, Mass., regarding Freeman's speculation in the art market and purchases of Italian paintings for Pickman, his progress on works commissioned by Pickman, and recent political events in Italy, 1848-1849. Among the works Freeman buys are paintings by Aga Caracci, Domenchino, Lutacelli, Raphael Mengs, Salvator Rosa, and Vanest. Freeman reports that he has completed his portrait of *Virginia* and is still painting a religious scene he refers to as *Two Marys*. In addition, Freeman describes the siege of Rome by French troops on July 3, 1849, and admits he is a liberal party sympathizer. Microfilm roll 3829, frames 959-989.

JOHN GADSBY CHAPMAN (1808-1889)
American painter, Florence and Rome, Italy

Four letters to [William Cullen] Bryant in New York, N.Y., November 1849-June 1869. While Chapman writes mostly about daily life, he requests an image of a profile of Bryant and a picture of an American apple tree to assist him with his painting. He says he will send copies of Roman newspapers so that Bryant may read about events in the United States from a Roman perspective. Microfilm roll N 5, frames 730-739. Originals in the New York Public Library, New York, N.Y.

JAMES CLAGHORN (1817-1884)
Art collector, Philadelphia, Pa.

Fifteen letters from artists in Florence and Rome, ca. 1850s. Included are letters from Hiram Powers, regarding the shipment of pictures; Peter Rothermel, describing his European travels; and William Whittredge, inquiring about Claghorn's sale of one of his works. In addition, there are 12 letters from Thomas Buchanan Read, who writes about his poetry, his apartment in Florence, his commissioned works for Claghorn, Napoleon III's rise to power, Hiram Powers and Randolph Rogers, and the prospects of war involving Austria, Russia, and Prussia. Microfilm roll 3580.

THOMAS BUCHANAN READ (1822-1872)
American painter, poet, Cincinnati, Ohio, and Rome and Florence, Italy

Correspondence between the Read family and notable artistic, literary, and political figures in Italy and the United States, 1850-1872 (ca. 45 items). In 20 letters to his sister Sarah and brother-in-law Cyrus Garrett, Read writes in detail about his paintings, patrons, exhibitions, family news, Hiram Powers, American society in Italy, and the success of his poem *The New Pastoral*. Included are ca. 10 letters from authors Nathaniel Hawthorne, Henry Wadsworth Longfellow, and Bayard Taylor, who writes from Pennsylvania on March 10, 1869, "You have your own delightful circle in Rome, with Longfellow, Appleton, the Grahams . . . Laurent Thompson, etc." Albert Bierstadt and Frederick Edwin Church each send a letter, complimenting Read on his paintings *Sheridan's Ride* and *Spirit of the Mist*, and Hiram Powers writes 5 letters from Florence. Also included are approximately 10 letters from Generals Philip H. Sheridan and William Sherman, August 28, 1869. In a letter to Philadelphia Union League Treasurer James Claghorn, Read writes about his poem and painting of Sheridan and his friends Ann Brewster, Harriet Hosmer, and Longfellow. Read's papers include ca. 20 responses to invitations from Robert Browning, Charlotte Cushman, Hosmer, Ernest Longfellow, Joseph Severn, and others. Also included are 3 items, in Italian, regarding Read's membership in the Associazione Artistica Internazionale; poems by David G. Adie, Luigi Dacconi, William W. Fosdick, Carlo Giorgio, Carlo Squaires, and Read; and a handwritten translation of an article about Read's 50th birthday celebration. Microfilm roll 1478.

Letters, notes, poems, and calling cards, 1850-1872 (ca. 220 items). Included are letters written by Read from Florence to friends in the United States, in which he writes of his poetry, family matters, daily life, painting commissions, friendship with Hiram Powers, and the death of his first wife and their daughter during the cholera epidemic, 1855. Letters to Read are from publishers, U.S. military personnel, artists in Rome including [Albert] Bierstadt and F[rederick] E[dwin] Church, and friends responding to social invitations and praising his poetry. Microfilm roll 1478, frames 385-1148. Originals privately owned.

Letter to Wayne MacVeagh, January 30, 1871. Read thanks MacVeagh for his letter and writes that he would have responded sooner had he not contracted a fever. He informs MacVeagh that he met with [General Philip H.] Sheridan in Naples. Microfilm roll P 24, frame 95. Originals in the Historical Society of Pennsylvania, Philadelphia, Pa.

WILLIAM PAGE (1811-1855)
American painter, Rome, Italy

Eight letters from Sarah Daugherty Page, Page's wife, primarily to her sisters in the United States, written while traveling in Italy with her husband, September 1850-January 1857. Sarah Page asks for family news, comforts her sister on the death of her son, and says she is homesick and does not like Italy, although her husband does. She writes about William's work, the possibilities for art commissions in Rome, the living arrangements in the old section of Florence, and her travels to Naples, where they climbed Mount Vesuvius with [Harriet] Hosmer and Miss Vaughan. Microfilm roll NY 59-10, frames 631-657.

Six letters from J.C. Hooker of Pakenham, Hooker & Co. in Rome, June 26, 1854-May 15, 1857. Hooker advises Page of the balances due on his account and informs him that he cannot make any more advances until he makes a deposit. On June 30, 1855, Hooker suggests that Page finish Crawford's portrait, asks why he has not painted for Quincy Shaw, and offers to give Page $10 a week from his own private funds until Page finds a way to pay his debt. He also writes that Mr. Story sends his regards and that Paris is a much nicer place to live than Rome. Microfilm roll 20, frames 537, 561, 571, 604, 630, 635.

Fifteen letters from friends in Italy and the United States, 1854-1856 and undated. Included are 6 letters from Robert and Elizabeth Browning in Florence in which they send an English translation of an essay titled "Tizian's Way of Painting" and write of everyday events and family matters, September 9, 1854-December 12, 1856. The Brownings inform Page that they like their painting but that there is a crack in it; they ask him to repair it before it gets worse. R[obert] S. Chilton of the Department of State in Washington, D.C., writes of his family and of [James Russell] Lowell's lectures on English poetry, February 10, 1855. Also included are 7 letters and short notes from Charlotte Cushman in England and Italy in which she writes that Page was not cordial to her when she visited him, asks if she did anything to cause the rift between them, and responds to Page's price of $600 for a painting by offering $400, August 22, 1855, and undated. Microfilm roll 1091, frames 1404-1408, 1420-1422, 1424-1431, 1438-1441. Originals privately owned.

Letter from Ednah D. Cheney responding to Sarah Page's requests for reminiscences of William Page, December 2, 1886 (8 pp.). Cheney mentions her travels abroad in 1864 and 1865 and meeting William Page in his studio in Rome. She describes his technique for applying color, notes how popular his drawings were among his fellow students, and lists some of the people whose portraits he painted. Microfilm roll 23, frames 3608-3620.

RANDOLPH ROGERS (1825-1892)
American sculptor, Italy

Documents relating to Rogers's life as an expatriate in Italy, ca. 1851-1892 (ca. 150 items). Included is an unpublished biography by his wife, Rosa G. Rogers, in which she describes his life in Italy (5 pp.); correspondence with Captain Montgomery C. Meigs regarding the *Life of Columbus* commission for the doors of the U.S. Capitol; letters to Professor Henry Simmons Frieze of the University of Michigan; 3 letters from Ferdinand von Muller; 1 letter from the Italian commissioner in which Rogers's knighthood is conferred; letters to his son, John Rogers, written after his death, from the Italian academies Perugia, Raffaello, and Romana (ca. 11 items). There are also a notebook, photographs, a datebook, loose sketches of studios and sculptures, 7 papers of agreements documenting commissions, a list of American artists living in Italy, and 2 sketchbooks of caricatures and Indian figures (ca. 52 pp.). Microfilm roll 501, frames 1-431. Originals in the Michigan Historical Collections, University of Michigan, Ann Arbor, Mich.

JOEL TANNER HART (1810-1877)
Sculptor, painter, poet, Florence, Italy

Letter to Joseph A. Humphreys in Paris, July 20, 1851. Hart writes that though Hiram Powers lent him some tools for his busts of Cicero and Mr. Clay, he still found the stone difficult to carve. He will find out if the busts can be cut with emery. He affirms that Humphreys left a good impression on the artists in Florence. Microfilm roll D 5, frames 126-128.

SOPHIA C. HITCHCOCK
Paris, France

Letter from Simon Stevens, introducing J. Augustus Beck, who is going to Italy to study sculptures by the Old Masters, July 4, 1854. Stevens asks Hitchcock to show Beck some of her own works as well as others to which she has access. Microfilm roll 20, frames 538-539.

HARRIET GOODHUE HOSMER (1830-1908)
American sculptor, Rome, Italy

Printed materials titled "Harriet Goodhue Hosmer: Collected Sources," consisting of pages photocopied from books, periodicals, encyclopedias, and newspapers, 1854-1973 (242 items). This material includes information about Hosmer's sculptures, her education in Rome under the English sculptor John Gibson, and her friendships with other American artists and writers living in Rome. Included are newspaper clippings from American newspapers that describe the exhibition of her sculpture *Zenobia*, 1865. Microfilm roll 1039, frames 59-1066. Originals in the Watertown Free Public Library, Watertown, Mass.

Two scrapbooks, 1859-1875 (93 items). Included are photographs of Hosmer, her sculpture, and portraits of her. Also included are certificates and diplomas from Italian organizations including Società delle Giovani Italiane, L'Accademia de'Quiriti, Società Promotrice d'Incoraggiamento alle Arti Industrie e Commercio, and Instituto

Italiano. Microfilm roll 1050, frames 93-193. Originals in the Watertown Free Public Library, Watertown, Mass.

"Harriet Hosmer: Her Era and Art," a master's thesis by Margaret Wendell LaBarre (1966, 295 pp.). LaBarre includes a biography, illustrations, and historical information about Hosmer's sculptures, and a chapter on "The Female Art Colony in Rome." Also included is an index to a thesis compiled by Joseph L. Curran, Jr., of the Watertown Free Public Library in 1973. Microfilm roll 1045, frames 797-1122. Original in the Watertown Free Public Library, Watertown, Mass.

SANFORD ROBINSON GIFFORD (1823-1880)
American painter, Europe
Three volumes of ca. 55 typed transcripts of lengthy letters, primarily to his father, from England, France, Germany, Greece, Italy, the Middle East, the Netherlands, and Switzerland, May 19, 1855-August 27, 1869. Gifford wrote 10 letters in the second volume during his extensive travels in Italy, describing the mountainous landscape, the people he met along the way, and hiking and sketching near the Italian-Swiss border, August 24, 1856-August 10, 1857. He writes in detail about monuments, buildings, cathedrals, museums, and works of art; notes that he has signed an 8-month lease on a studio in Rome; and reports that a pickpocket tried to steal his notebook in Milan. He says he attends social and cultural events including parties, the opera, a country fair, the Carnival in Rome, and Holy Week festivities. He mentions other American artists and writers, including [Edward Sheffield] Bartholomew, [Joseph] Mozier, [Hiram] Powers, [Peter Frederick] Rothermel, Harriet Beecher Stowe, and Eugene Warburg, and writes of his travels with [Albert] Bierstadt. He also asks for news and letters from home. Included in vol. 3 are 4 letters written while in Italy, July 12, 1868-August 11, 1868. Gifford writes that he crossed into Val d'Aosta by Mount Blanc on a mule, climbed the Matterhorn and Monte Rosa, and went through the Saint Bernardino Pass. He mentions sketching, family matters, and the magnificent views. Included are 3 additional letters from Rome, October 19, 1868-January 8, 1869. Gifford writes that he has settled into a comfortable apartment and has visited ancient ruins and the Villa d'Este in Tivoli. He also mentions that he has sketched, visited friends, gone for long walks, and shopped for supplies in Rome with [Jervis] McEntree. Microfilm roll D 21, frames not numbered.

Sketchbook (ca. 110 pp.) and passport (ca. 65 pp.) from travels in Italy, 1856-1857. The sketchbook includes drawings of monuments, figures, landscapes, animals, and [Albert] Bierstadt sketching at Piccola Marina, Capri. The passport is stamped from cities in Italy and elsewhere in Europe. Microfilm roll 688, frames 229-303, 525-559. Originals privately owned.

Diary of Mary Louise Willard, wife of Gifford's nephew, kept while she traveled through Europe, February 27-August 1888 (ca. 103 pp.). Italian cities that Willard visited include Capri, Florence, Genoa, Lucerne, Milan, Naples, Pisa, Pompeii, Rome, and Venice. She writes about the works of art she saw and includes a ledger of travel expenses and an itinerary of cities, works, and monuments to be seen. Microfilm roll 688, frames 571-625. Original privately owned.

JOHN ROWSON SMITH (1810-1864)
Painter, New York, N.Y.

Booklet to accompany the exhibition in New York of a panorama painting of Europe, 1855. Smith describes and explains what people will see on his 30,000 square feet of canvas showing 100 different views of Europe. (An image of the painting is not included on the microfilm.) The booklet reads much like a travel guide and describes sights in Antwerp, Berlin, Brussels, Hamburg, Paris, and Rouen. Considerable attention is given to Italy, especially Florence, Milan, Naples, Pompeii, Rome, Terni, Tivoli, and Venice. Smith offers general travel advice; population counts; and historical accounts of major buildings, monuments, and conditions in which the citizens of these European cities live. Microfilm roll N 46, frames 791-816. Originals in the New York Public Library, New York, N.Y.

THOMAS WATERMAN WOOD (1823-1903)
American painter, Italy

Diary kept mainly while in Paris but also while in Genoa, Rome, Florence, and Milan, January 1-August 13, 1859 (228 pp.). Wood traveled to Paris with his wife, Minnie, and lived in an apartment but also maintained a separate studio in which he worked daily. He writes of sketching in Rome, working on specific paintings, and searching for and hiring models. He also comments on the French soldiers in Italy and his favorable impression of Genoa. Included are references to his associations with [Peter] Rothermel and with Mr. and Mrs. Welsch. Microfilm roll 2809, frames 1064-1178. Originals owned by the Thomas Waterman Wood Art Gallery, Montpelier, Vt.

JOHN NEAL TILTON (1860-1924?)
American Architect, Chicago, Ill.

Scrapbook including photographs and newspaper clippings from Italy, Scotland, Switzerland, Gibraltar, the Nile River, and New York State, 1860s-1870s and undated (ca. 225 items). Included are photographs of buildings, piazzas, monuments, landscapes, drawings, and paintings as well as portrait photographs of [Thomas] Carlyle, W[illiam] W[etmore] Story, [Alfred, Lord] Tennyson, and John Rollin Tilton. There are also photographs of ancient sculptures, works by American sculptor E[mma] S[tebbins], the view outside of Tilton's window in Rome, and of the interior of his grandmother's home, also in Rome. Microfilm roll 2082, frames 1003-1097.

ANDREW LONGACRE (1831-1906)
American engraver, Italy, France, and North Africa

Sketchbook kept while in Italy, France, and North Africa, ca. 1861-1894 (33 pp. plus 10 loose sketches). Included are landscapes, figures, Roman coins, and scenes of Florence done in pencil and in watercolor. Microfilm roll 986.

WILLIAM HENRY RINEHART (1825-1874)
American sculptor, Rome, Italy
Bound volume containing sketchbooks, financial documents, correspondence with patrons, and papers relating to the disposition of Rinehart's estate, 1861-1875 (ca. 250 items). Included are 12 letters from Rinehart to patron William T. Walters discussing Americans in Rome, a cholera epidemic, the 1867 Paris exhibition, progress on commissioned works, and the shipment of works to Walters, 1867-1874. Rinehart's patron John W. Paine writes 21 letters regarding the commissions for a bronze memorial statue and a bust, 1872-1874. Included are 5 letters to Walters from Charles Coleman, Louis Lang of the Rome banking house Maquay and Hooker, George Simonds, and Edward Swilte, describing Rinehart's last days and his funeral in Rome. Also included are 28 letters from W.H. Herriman to Walters regarding the completion of Rinehart's unfinished commissions and the disposition of his possessions, 1874-1880, and 6 letters from Paine addressed "Dear Sir," which are probably to Herriman. There are also a priced inventory of marble works in Rinehart's studio and a priced catalog, in Italian, of an auction of his works. Included in the unbound papers are bills, accounts, receipts, sketchbooks, notebooks, a copy of Rinehart's will, 2 inventories, and 1 photograph of Rinehart. Microfilm roll 3116.

ISABELLA STEWART GARDNER (1840-1924)
Art collector, Boston, Mass.

Files concerning her purchases of paintings, antiques, furniture, statues, architectural details, decorative arts, jewelry, etc., ca. 1862-1923 (ca. 1,300 items), arranged alphabetically by dealer's name. Files may contain letters, canceled checks, invoices, notes, receipts, etc. Many of her purchases were from Italian dealers or involved works by Italian artists. Some of the dealers were Stefano Bardini, V. Barone, Dino Borozzi, Antonio Carrer, Francesco Dorigo, M. Jesurum, Gaetano Pepe, Consiglio Ricchetti, and Moise Dalla Torre. There is also a large file on Fernand Robert, a Paris exporter. Microfilm rolls 631-632.

BAILY AND COMPANY
Philadelphia, Pa.

Booklet concerning a mosaic sent to the United States from the ruins of Paestum, an ancient city south of Naples, and exhibited by Baily and Company, 1865 (16 pp.). While the subject of the mosaic is not described, the writer discusses the development of mosaic as an art form and gives a brief history of Paestum. Microfilm roll N 38, frames 423-431. Originals in the New York Public Library, New York, N.Y.

EDWARD DARLEY BOIT (1840-1915)
American art patron, painter, Italy

Letters written in diary form and sent weekly to his parents while he traveled in England, France, Switzerland, Germany, and Italy, 1866-1867 (267 pp.). He writes of buildings, paintings, monuments, travel details, and shopping trips. Microfilm roll 83, frames 105-454. Originals privately owned.

Visitors' book, containing signatures, notes, and poems from friends and relatives who visited Cernitoio, Boit's home in Italy, between 1901 and 1914 (46 pp.). Visitors included Robert Browning, Henry James, and Joseph Lindon Smith. Microfilm roll 2395, frames 271-298.

Three pocket diaries kept while living at Cernitoio, 1901-1904 (209 pp.), 1904-1906 (190 pp.), 1906-1907 (144 pp.). Boit keeps records of the weather and writes about friends, family activities, social events, and travels in Italy. Microfilm roll 83, frames 794-900, 902-997, 999-1071. Originals privately owned.

L.G. DARLEY (Mrs. Felix O.C. Darley)
American artist's wife, France and Italy

Pocket diary kept while on a trip to Italy and France, January-June 1867 (ca. 189 pp.). L.G. Darley writes of sight-seeing and shopping trips with other artists' wives, occasionally mentions that her husband is painting, and reports that they see other American artists including [Thomas] Ball, [Hiram] Powers, and [Elihu] Vedder. Microfilm roll D 177, frames 118-213. Originals privately owned.

VINNIE REAM HOXIE (1847-1914)
American sculptor, Rome, Italy

Typescript of an unpublished biography titled "Vinnie and Her Friends," by Harold E. Miner (392 pp. plus notes and illustrations). Subtitled "The Daughter of the Capitol," chapter 8 discusses her travels in Europe and her studies in Florence and Rome, ca. 1869-1870. Microfilm roll 297, frames 1166-1611.

ELIHU VEDDER (1836-1923)
American symbolist painter, author, Rome and Isle of Capri, Italy

Papers relating to Vedder's career in Rome, including family and professional correspondence, 1867-1923; diaries and journal notes, 1878-1890; notes, manuscripts, and several hundred handwritten original and typed copies of essays and poems; family legal and financial papers; and clippings, catalogs, and miscellaneous material (ca. 5,000 items). Correspondence includes letters from Vedder and his wife Caroline (Carrie) Rosekrans to their parents and family, and correspondence with friends, patrons, and publishers, such as Charles Coleman, Kate Field, W. Lewis Frazer, William Graham, William and Elizabeth Herriman, Houghton and Mifflin, William Dean Howells, J.J. Jarves, William Laffin, Francis Davis Millet, J.P. Morgan, George Simonds, Stanford White, Henry D. Williams, and George Yewell. Microfilm rolls 515-526.

Carrie Vedder's diary, kept while in Rome, records her husband's travels and work; the deaths of Victor Emmanuel and Pope Pius IX; the aftermath of a libel scandal with *L'Art* magazine; and her social outings with friends, including Elizabeth Boott, Anne Brewster, Edward Haskell, Mr. and Mrs. Herriman, Mr. and Mrs. Chauncy Ives, William J. Stillman, Mr. and Mrs. William Story, the Trollopes, and others, January-December 1878 (microfilm roll 526, frames 96-278). In addition, Carrie Vedder kept a record of the Vedders' travels in the United States, February 3-November 2, 1882 (9 pp.), and Elihu Vedder maintained a diary-sketchbook during his voyage on the Nile River, November 25, 1889-March 5, 1890 (ca. 100 pp.) (microfilm roll 526, frames 279ff.). Vedder also recorded the dates of his travels in a separate log titled "Nile Journey and Dates" (ca. 5 pp.). Microfilm rolls 526-528 feature notes, drawings, illustrations, and typescripts for Vedder's books and several hundred essays and poems by Vedder and others. Family papers include financial and legal documents, such as wills, diplomas, insurance certificates, records of sales of Vedder's works, 1856-1907, and statements of accounts with galleries including New York's Macbeth and Parke Bernet and the Rome banking house Maquay and Hooker (roll 528). Microfilm rolls 515-529.

Photographs including 55 images of him, 131 of his family, and 157 of his works, ca. 1866-1913 (457 items). Microfilm roll 671, frames 1-614.

Correspondence with friends and artists while he lived in Rome, 1869-1923 (ca. 130 letters). Included are letters from Anne Brewster, Onorato Carlandi, Jesse Carter, the Century Association, Timothy Cole, Robert Swain Gifford, John La Farge, Charles F. McKim, Francis Davis Millet, Auguste Rodin, and William Wetmore Story. Microfilm roll 2323.

Papers, 1877-1922, including correspondence between Vedder's wife, Caroline (Carrie) Rosekrans, and Mrs. L.G. Bagnell of Perpigon, France (ca. 15 items). There are also reviews, magazine articles, newspaper clippings, a letter from painter Ali Ben Haggin, a letter from author Nathan Haskell Dole, and ca. 250 poems written by Vedder or dedicated to Vedder by friends, including several by Francis B. Keene. Vedder's guest register, kept in Italy from 1897 to 1914, includes the date, name, and address of each guest. There are also excerpts from his published autobiography *Digressions of V.*(1910), including notes for the preface; a first edition of Edward FitzGerald's *Rubaiyat of Omar Khayyam* (1859), and a list of paintings and reproductions by Vedder that are for sale, with size and price for each title. Microfilm rolls NAA 3-NAA 5. Originals in the American Academy of Arts and Letters, New York, N.Y.

Two letters from Vedder in Rome. The first, addressed to "Madam," thanks her for her poem based on one of his works and announces a new set of reproductions, September 7, 1884. The second, to Mr. Bull of *Century Magazine,* concerns the publication of Vedder's "Verses," September 4, 1909. Microfilm roll N 8, frames 934-939. Originals in the New York Public Library, New York, N.Y.

Sketches, done mostly in Rome, 1885-1890 (ca. 85 items). The works include landscapes, figure and drapery studies, a photograph of Charles Keck's sculpture *Fountain Boy* (after drawings by Vedder), a commissioned design for a Tiffany stained-glass window, and preparatory studies for paintings, including *Soul in Bondage* and *Morning Glory*. The sketches are in a variety of media, including pencil, crayon, chalk, and tempera. Microfilm roll NCUD-22. Originals in the Cooper Union Museum Drawings Collection.

Two letters to Horace Thomson Carpenter, New York, N.Y., December 27, 1903, and Sorrento, June 14, 1904. Vedder describes his pleasure in moving into Fortuny's old studio, proposes a drawing trip through Italy, and informs Carpenter that he is sending proofs of photographs to him and making photographs and reproductions to take to Capri. Microfilm roll P 14, frames 407-408. Originals in the Philadelphia Museum of Art, Philadelphia, Pa.

Papers relating to an exhibition of his work organized by the Macbeth Gallery, New York, N.Y., February-March, 1912 (ca. 20 items). Included are 15 letters from Vedder and his daughter Anita in Rome regarding the preparations and the success of the exhibition; 1 price list, titled "Reproductions of Works by Elihu Vedder"; a lengthy invitation list of friends and patrons; a catalog of the show at Boston's Doll and Richards Gallery; and 9 financial documents, including customs and shipping invoices. Microfilm roll NMc 11, frames 1091-1164.

Photographs, undated, including 2 images of Vedder and his works in a studio and photographs of sculptress Enid Yandell. Microfilm roll 2768, frames 680.

CONSTANTINO BRUMIDI (1805-1880)
Italian-American painter, Washington, D.C.

Booklet by Samuel Douglas Wyeth about Brumidi's *Apotheosis of Washington* (1868) in the U.S. Capitol. The booklet summarizes Brumidi's biography and describes and explains the allegorical figures in the fresco. Microfilm roll N 52, frames 960-966. Originals in the New York Public Library, New York, N.Y.

JOHN QUINCY ADAMS WARD (1830-1910)
Sculptor, New York, N.Y.

Ca. 15 letters from friends and artists in Italy, 1869-1890. In 2 letters [Jommoro?] Gagliardi, Carrara, writes that he will begin carving Ward's statue in the best marble he can find as soon as he receives the model from Ward, January 2, 1869, and January

7, 1869. He also includes a list of expenses and says it will cost $6,000 for the marble, the labor, the studio space rental, and the transportation of the statue to the United States. In 11 letters from Florence and Carrara, Robert Cushing keeps Ward informed of the progress made on Ward's marble statue. Cushing says that he and Gagliardi have selected the best block of marble and describes the preparations to ship the statue in a watertight case to New York. Included is 1 shipping contract issued for the transport of 1 statue from Italy to New York by Maquay, Hooker & Co., July 12, 1871. John Swinton writes that he has been in Rome for 6 weeks but has been ill, April 14, 1890. Microfilm roll 509, frames 729-731, 818-841, 899, 896-912. Originals in the New-York Historical Society, New York, N.Y.

JULIAN ALDEN WEIR (1852-1919)
American painter, Paris, France, and Connecticut

Typescript copies of correspondence between John F. Weir, Julian's brother, and their father Robert, 1869-1880. In his letters sent from Rome, John F. Weir encourages Julian to study in Italy, 1869. Included are letters to Weir from J. Wencker while in Rome regarding their friends [Filadelfo] Simi and Mr. and Mrs. William Wetmore Story, 1877. Also included is a letter from John Twachtman in Cincinnati, Ohio, discussing Frank Duveneck's invitation to study in Italy, 1880. Twachtman confesses his ambitions, saying: "You do not know how tempting every opportunity is to me and how I long to go in quest of fame and fortune." Microfilm roll 71.

Typescript of a letter from Joseph Wencker, in French, November 14, 1877. Wencker thanks him for his letter, writes of mutual friends including [Filadelfo] Simi who is also in Rome, and reports that he is no longer proficient in English. Microfilm roll 71, frame 1001.

FRANKLIN SIMMONS (1839-1913)
American sculptor, Rome, Italy

Sixteen letters to Professor Waterman T. Hewett of Cornell University, 1872-1913. Simmons writes about family matters, mutual friends' activities, and sculptures on which he is working. In a 1904 letter he observes that many Americans have left Rome. Microfilm roll P 14, frames 287-302. Originals in the Philadelphia Museum of Art, Philadelphia, Pa.

Brief note to J.B. Brown and Sons in Portland, Maine, in which Simmons asks for a "draft of London," August 12, 1889. Microfilm roll P 22, frame 452. Originals in the Historical Society of Pennsylvania, Philadelphia, Pa.

JOHN ROLLIN TILTON (1828-1888)
Landscape painter, Boston, Mass.

Undated letter and newspaper clipping, 1873. Tilton writes to an unnamed friend saying that he is eager to return to Rome and regrets bringing his pictures to the United States. The clipping describes the technique used in his painting *The Temple of Kom Ombos* on display at the Royal Academy. Microfilm roll DDU 1, frames 740-742.

MOSES JACOB EZEKIEL (1844-1917)
American sculptor, Rome, Italy

Typed manuscript, with editorial notes, titled "Memories of the Baths of Diocletian," about his life up to 1912 (612 pp.). He writes of his childhood in Richmond, Va.; his education at the Virginia Military Institute; his first training in art; his experiences as a Confederate soldier on the battlefield during the Civil War; and travels to Berlin and France before going to Rome in 1874, where he spent most of his adult life. In Rome, he describes his studios, including one on the ground floor of the Baths of Diocletian. He also writes of his works, commissions, a public exhibition of his work, making a bust of [Franz von] Liszt, and his impressions of buildings and piazzas. He describes his friendships with General Custis Lee, Elihu Vedder, and General Ulysses S. Grant, and says he is generally acquainted with royalty and cardinals. He talks of assisting in restoring the Villa d'Este and its fountains in order to sell the Villa for the owners and of accompanying Emperor Wilhelm and the empress to the Villa. In addition to daily activities, he mentions going to the Masonic Lodge, the arrival of family members in Rome in 1906, and preparations for the 1911 World Exhibition celebrating the 50th anniversary of the proclamation of the kingdom of Italy. Included are ca. 10 illustrations of people he knew and of some of his works. Microfilm roll 969, frames 437-1155. Originals in the American Jewish Archives, Cincinnati, Ohio.

Letter to Miss Early, January 18, 1910, and 1 letter to his brother Henry, September 4, 1913, both written from Rome. Ezekiel tells Miss Early that her "By Ways of Virginia History" has arrived, thanks her for it, and says it is appropriate for him as he still has the Confederate flag and the coat of arms of the Old Dominion in his studio at the Baths of Diocletian. He writes Henry from the Piazza di Spagna, noting that he went for a walk with Oscar and bought a coin at an antique shop. Microfilm roll DDU 1, frames 164-168.

Fifty-one photographs including 1 of Ezekiel seated in a garden, 1 of him in a dining cabin on board a steamship, ca. 1910, and 7 of his studio in Rome. Others include Ezekiel's statues, bas reliefs, and busts. Microfilm roll 847, frames 543-644.

MARY CASSATT (1845-1926)
American artist, Italy

Three letters to Emily Sartain while Cassatt was traveling through Italy, May 25-November 26, 1874. Cassatt writes from Parma and Rome about her artistic improvement, her disappointment with Parma, and her difficulty in finding an available model in Rome. Microfilm roll 3658, frames 1040-1043, 1047. Originals in the Pennsylvania Academy of the Fine Arts, Philadelphia, Pa.

FRANCIS DAVIS MILLET (1846-1912)
American painter, Venice and Rome, Italy

A letter to Frederick Chapman, Venice, December 25, 1874, describes his life there. Another, to James Hunt, January 20, 1912, tells of his recent experiences at the American Academy in Rome. Microfilm roll NAA-2, frames 456-457, 591-595. Originals in the American Academy of Arts and Letters, New York, N.Y.

TRUMAN SEYMOUR (1824-1891)
American soldier, artist, Italy

Six sketchbooks kept while he lived in Italy, of landscapes, monuments, copies of masters and architectural details, 1876-1891. Included is a ca. 60-pp. sketchbook begun on May 25, 1879, illustrated with copies of Old Masters, beside which are written descriptions of the painting (frames 617-647). The subjects Seymour sketched are from Italy, North Africa, Spain, Switzerland, and France; those done in Italy consist mostly of Renaissance art. Microfilm roll 942, frames 434-798. Originals privately owned.

Five sketchbooks kept while he traveled throughout Italy, specifically, Rome, Venice, and a number of other cities and towns, 1880-1883 (ca. 275 pp.). The penciled sketches depict churches, landscapes, villas, and panoramic views as well as architectural details such as columns and facades. Most of the sketches are labeled with location and date. Microfilm roll 1038, frames 135-449. Originals privately owned.

JOHN SARTAIN (1808-1897)
English miniaturist, engraver, Philadelphia, Pa.

Certificates and letters from organizations in France and Italy conferring artistic and humanitarian awards on Sartain, 1878-1887 (33 items). Awards from Italy include certificates from the Instituto Italico del Progresso, Società Internazionale d'-Incoraggiamento, Associazione dei Salvatori, and the Società Umanitaria dei Salvatori Italiani. A letter from Antonio Padula of the Sourindro Morun Tagore in Genoa honors Sartain for virtuosity in lithography and asks him to arrange for James Bertrand Payen-Payne to be considered for an honorary doctor of laws degree. Microfilm roll P 24, frames 42-87. Originals in the Historical Society of Pennsylvania, Philadelphia, Pa.

JAMES MCNEILL WHISTLER (1834-1903)
American painter, Venice, Italy

Three letters regarding his study in Venice with Frank Duveneck's circle, 1879-1880. Whistler writes to his mother about the cold winter, his pastel work, the suitability of the city for painters, and people including [William] Graham and Mrs. Harris, wife of the American consul. In 2 letters from Whistler and his wife in London to the American artist Otto Henry Bacher in Venice, Whistler expresses a desire to acquire some of Bacher's etchings, mentions the engagement of Miss Blott and Lord Colin Campbell, describes the success of an exhibition of his etchings created in Venice and the envy of his competitors, and sends "love to all the Boys and the old man (Duveneck), dear old thing" (ca. 1880). Microfilm roll 456. Originals in the Freer Gallery of Art, Smithsonian Institution, Washington, D.C.

Six photographs of works completed by Whistler in Venice, 1879-1880. Microfilm roll 2082.

THOMAS RIDGEWAY GOULD (1818-1881)
American sculptor, Florence, Italy

Letter to literary critic Edwin P[ercy] Whipple, April 11, 1880. Gould writes that he is grieved by Matthew's death and recalls the time Matthew and his brother, Augustus, visited him in Boston. He reports that Matthew aged physically in the last 2 years but retained a beautiful and youthful spirit. Microfilm roll DDU 1, frames 219-221.

JOHN HENRY TWACHTMAN (1853-1902)
Painter, Cincinnati, Ohio, and New Bedford, Mass.

Three letters to an unknown recipient, 1880. Twachtman writes that he will be going to Florence in 1 month because [Frank] Duveneck has offered him a teaching position at his private school. Microfilm roll 71, frames 1014-1016.

ALEXANDER DRAKE (1843-1916)
Wood engraver, New York, N.Y.

Two letters from Robert Blum in Venice, August 10, 1881, and undated. In the first, Blum writes a letter of introduction for Mr. Hodges of St. Louis, whose article on Venetian life Drake illustrated. The second letter concerns the arrival of a drawing from Italy, sent by Blum to Drake. Microfilm roll 3582, frames 873, 865. Originals privately owned.

HENRY HOBSON RICHARDSON (1838-1886)
Architect, Brookline, Mass.

Eight letters to his wife, Julia, while he was traveling in France, England, Italy, and Spain, June 22-September 11, 1882. Each letter contains several entries written over the course of several days. In 2 entries written from Genoa and Venice, Richardson writes about his companions and how the traveling has tired him, July 30 and August 12. He writes 1 letter from a gondola in Venice and describes the gondoliers' costumes. He notes that he liked Ravenna, that there is a great deal to study at Saint Mark's, that he went to vespers there, and that he goes to the piazza of Saint Mark's in the evenings to have coffee and listen to the band. Microfilm roll 643, frames 302-310.

TIMOTHY COLE (1852-1931)
American engraver, Italy

Letters to his employers at *Century Magazine*, New York, N.Y., July 1884-1892 (114 items). Cole writes in detail about the paintings he is engraving for Italian museums, inquires about woodblocks he has mailed to New York, and says he is willing to work for *Century Magazine* for another year on the same terms as the previous year. He also writes about his tools, his techniques, the small number of artists in Florence due to a cholera epidemic, and his preference for making engravings from original paintings rather than from photographs. Microfilm roll D 117, frames 194-489, 507.

HERMON ATKINS MACNEIL (1866-1947)
American sculptor, Rome, Italy

Papers, 1885-1947, including several sketchbooks with notes kept while he was a Rinehart Scholar in Italy, 1896-1900. Papers include sketches, detailed measurements, and notes of various monuments, buildings, and figures in Florence, Frascati, Ravenna, Rome, Tivoli, Venice, and Verese. Included is an illustrated booklet titled *Quindici Tabole di Ornamentazione Policroma del Secolo XIII*. Microfilm rolls 2726-2727.

Biographical material concerning Augustus Saint-Gaudens's recommendation of MacNeil, and MacNeil's subsequent acceptance of the Rinehart Scholarship for sculpture in Rome, 1896-1900. Microfilm roll 503, frames 981-982. Microfilm roll D 34, frame 780.

OTTO HENRY BACHER (1857-1909)
Painter, etcher, author, Venice, Italy

His papers contain a drawing of "Caricatures of Some of the Venetian Group of 1886" by Robert Blum, and an etching of Venice by Theodore M. Wendel. Microfilm roll 1654, frames 369-371.

BERNARD BERENSON (1865-1959)
American art critic, Boston, Mass., and Florence, Italy

Ca. 1,200 letters from Berenson to Isabella Stewart Gardner, chronicling Berenson's efforts to collect Old Master paintings for Gardner's museum at Fenway Court in Boston, 1887-1924. As Gardner's protégé following his graduation from Harvard in 1887, Berenson comments on his visits to various European cities, suggests books for Gardner to read, reflects upon Venetian and other Italian Renaissance artists, and reveals his own developing sense of knowledge and criticism. Berenson's letters document arrangements for the purchases of works, including Botticelli's *The Death of Lucretia*; Gainsborough's *Blue Boy*; Titian's *The Rape of Europa*; Velásquez's *The Riva degli Schiavoni*; Van Dyck's *A Lady with a Rose*; Rembrandt's *A Lady and Gentleman in Black*; Dürer's *Portrait of a Man*; Giotto's *Presentation of the Christ Child*; and other works by Fra Angelico, Bellini, Giorgione, Holbein, Rubens, Tintoretto, and Titian. Several letters from Berenson's wife, Mary, acknowledge Berenson's controversial reputation among other dealers and collectors but attempt to restore Gardner's confidence in him. Microfilm rolls 696-698. Originals in the Isabella Stewart Gardner Museum, Boston, Mass.

HENRY H. HARRAL
Folkestone, England

Letter to John Sartain, October 18, 1886. Harral says he will go to Italy to find American artists willing to show their work in "The American Exhibition" in London, 1887, and that only sculptors Larkin G. Mead and William G. Turan have agreed to send works. He notes that he is enclosing a list (not present) of American sculptors and painters working in Florence and will send a list of artists in Rome. As a guard for the exhibition, he recommends an Englishman he believes to be trustworthy and experienced. Microfilm roll P 28, frame 179. Original in the Historical Society of Pennsylvania, Philadelphia, Pa.

ROBERT FREDERICK BLUM (1857-1903)
American painter, illustrator, Venice, Italy

Ten letters to William Merritt Chase, 1887-1888 and undated. Blum illustrates his letters with water scenes and figures and writes about travels, mutual acquaintances, and other artists including [Frank] Duveneck, [John Henry] Twachtman, and [James McNeill] Whistler. Microfilm roll N 68-101, frames 3-81. Originals in the Chapellier Galleries Collection, New York, N.Y.

Three undated letters from Venice to Miss Minnie, Miss Virginia, and an unknown recipient. In the illustrated letters Blum writes of his surroundings and social matters. He also mentions that the Americans in Venice went to the Lido for the Fourth of July and that [William Merritt] Chase had his portrait painted by Whistler. Microfilm roll D 8, frames 340-348.

ROBERT REID (1862-1929)
American artist, Italy and France

Ca. 20 letters and postcards to his sister, Sara Reid, and 2 letters to his uncle written during travel in Italy, January 10-February 27, 1887. Reid visited Capri, Genoa, Naples, Paestum, Pompeii, Rome, Turin, and Venice. He writes about the weather, his love for Venice, the works of art he sees, and his anxiety about the upcoming Paris Salon, at which he hopes to exhibit his work done at the Julian Academy. Microfilm roll 641, frames 1-509.

CHARLES HENRY HART (1847-1918)
Lawyer, New York, N.Y.

Letter to N.E. Janney from P.M. Kennedy regarding collector W.T. Bishop's sale of the painting, *Assumption of the Virgin* by Ludovico Caracci, August 12, 1888. Microfilm roll 928, frame 528.

IRA LAKE (1865-1954)
American sculptor, Rome, Italy

Diary kept in Rome, August 19, 1888-March 7, 1889 (218 pp.) Extensive, daily entries are almost illegible. There are pen-and-ink sketches. Not microfilmed.

ALBERT KAHN (1869-1942)
Architect, Detroit, Mich.

Ca. 375 photographs, 1888-1941 and mostly undated, documenting his career as an architect and his travels abroad. There are 54 photographs of Kahn and 30 of his wife, Ernestine, and their children, Lydia and Edgar. Also included are 31 signed photographs of his friends, including 5 photographs of Kahn and his wife with Diego Rivera in front of one of Rivera's murals. There are 10 photographs of Kahn and his wife on a ship bound for Europe, and ca. 125 photographs of buildings, churches, and scenes in Spain and Italy that Kahn took while he was traveling through Florence, Pisa, Rome, Todi, and other cities and towns. Microfilm roll 1114, frames 239-681.

ROBERT HENRI (1865-1929)
American painter, Italy

Diary of travel in Italy, November 19-December 2, 1890 (128 pp.). Henri writes in detail about his daily activities, including sight-seeing visits to Roman churches, monuments, catacombs, and art collections. He reports getting lost in Perugia and traveling to Florence, where he meets artists Porter and Scanlon. Henri describes various churches and galleries, criticizes tourists and amateur artists who copy Old Master works, and reviews at length paintings at the Uffizi, writing: "It is a wonderful collection and a wonderful opportunity for us fellows who aspire to be artists ourselves." Microfilm roll 885, frames 526-590. Restricted access. Use requires prior permission.

Notebook-sketchbook documenting his travels in Chioggia, Lotto Marino, and Venice, August 29-September 12, 1891 (33 pp.). Henri describes his fondness for Lotto Marino, writing: "It's a place to make an artist go wild over color and character." He refers to sketches by his friend [Italico] Brass, the Austrian painter whom he met as a student at [Adolphe William] Bouguereau's studio in Paris. While in Venice, he writes about the cafés and the street life and describes his train ride to Etaples, France. There are lists of expenses and of items to purchase in Italy, in addition to figure studies and pencil-and-ink sketches. Not microfilmed.

JOSEPH LINDON SMITH (1863-1950)
Painter, Boston, Mass.

Pamphlet containing text of a lecture given to the Boston Art Students' League, 1892, on Renaissance Venetian painters. Artists discussed are Gentile Bellini, Carpaccio, Cima da Conegliano, Giorgione, Moroni, Tintoretto, Titian, Bonifazio [Veronese], [Paolo] Veronese, and Vivarini (6 pp.). Smith talks about color, landscape, and line as well as influence from Byzantium and encourages his audience to go to museums to study the Old Masters. Microfilm roll N 47, frames 252-256. Originals in the New York Public Library, New York, N.Y.

THOMAS BALL (1819-1911)
American sculptor, Florence, Italy

Letter to Charles Henry Hart, April 6, 1893, informing him that, in accord with Hart's wish, he is sending one of his miniatures for inclusion in an exhibition of "retrospective painters." Microfilm roll D 5, frames 5-6.

Letter to J.S. Dwight in Boston, May 21, 1893. Ball congratulates Dwight on his 80th birthday and discusses a bust of Johann Sebastian Bach on which he is working. As Ball has no visual source on which to base his likeness of Bach, he says he has relied upon inspiration from Bach's music. Microfilm roll P 22, frame 31. Originals in the Historical Society of Pennsylvania, Philadelphia, Pa.

CHARLES LANG FREER (1856-1919)
Art collector, Detroit, Mich.

Ca. 30 letters to Colonel Frank J. Hecker, collector and artist, written during Freer's journeys in Europe and Southeast Asia, 1894-1906. Freer describes his visits to Italian cities and villages and reports his purchases of bottles and several Renaissance terra-cotta sculptures and his plans to attend the 1901 Venice exhibition. On October 9, 1894, Freer writes that James McNeill Whistler's *Little Venice* "is more beautiful than Venice itself seen from the same view." Microfilm roll 455.

AMERICAN ACADEMY IN ROME
New York and Rome

Records of the New York office, 1894-1974 (62 ft.). Included is the correspondence of presidents Charles McKim and William Rutherford Mead with many other architects about the creation and development of the Academy. These letters concern such matters as the establishment of the American School of Architecture, educational requirements to be an architect, educational philosophies, the course of study, selection of students, inclusion of painters and sculptors, rules and regulations for the fellows, fund raising, selection of directors, salaries, allocation of space in the school, progress of the fellows, purchases of buildings, incorporation by the U.S. Congress, consolidation with the American School of Classical Studies, etc. In addition there are files on Frank Millet, George Breck, William M. Kendall, Gorham Stevens, C. Grant La Farge, Roscoe Guernsey, Charles Platt, James C. Egbert, H. Blakiston Wilkins, John Russell Pope, James Monroe Hewlett, Chester Holmes Aldrich, James Kellum Smith, and A.W. Van Buren. Correspondents include William Howland Blashfield, William Boring, Daniel Burnham, Jesse Benedict Carter, Frederick Crowninshield, Frank Miles Day, Daniel Chester French, Austin Lord, H. Siddons Mowbray, Elihu Root, Henry Walters, et al. There are also various other forms of records, including applications, minutes, photographs, newsletters, legal documents, etc. Not microfilmed.

Annual records of the American Academy in Rome, published by the New York office, 1911-1940, 1943-1951, 1955-1959. Many reports are at least 50 pp., and they regularly contain the following information: reports of the director, librarian, treasurer, and executive committee; announcements of new fellows; lists of past and present fellows, trustees, officers, and associates; copies of the Academy charter and act of incorporation; photographs of student work; and news about excursions, competitions, and exhibitions. The reports give detailed information about Academy activities in the context of the political, social, and artistic life of Rome. Microfilm rolls ItRO 2, 3, 11, 12.

Records of the Rome office, 1912-1931 (2 ft.), mainly the administrative correspondence of Gorham Stevens, director of the School of Fine Art, including letters from artists Moses Ezekiel, Edwin H. Blashfield, George de Forest Brush, Paul Manship, et al. Not microfilmed.

Papers relating to the election of new Academy fellows (9 items). Included are 3 typed press releases (1931, 1938, and date illegible); 1 published circular, titled "Annual Announcement of Fellowships of the School of Fine Arts"; and 5 newspaper clippings on the Prix de Rome, 1940-1942. Microfilm roll N 121, frames 163-175.

GEORGE de FOREST BRUSH (1855-1941)
American painter, Florence, Italy

Undated letter to Emma Thayer, wife of artist Abbott H. Thayer, from Pisticci, Italy. Brush writes of his friends saying Gerald has made great progress and reports that Robert is skillful at drawing. Microfilm roll D 200, frames 943-944.

Photographs and biographical material relating to Brush and his family in Florence, ca. 1896-1915. Ca. 15 photographs depict Brush, his family, and friends, 1896-1908. Included are brief notes about Brush in Italy written by his daughter, Nancy Douglas Bowditch, in preparation for her biography of him, *The Joyous Painter* (1970). Also included is Barry Faulkner's biographical sketch of Brush mentioning their experience together in Florence and Rome while he was a student at the American Academy. Microfilm roll 2830.

"If this eager searcher after knowledge cannot get a job as architect after three years of adventurous research in Italy he may be taken on as window washer in the office section of one of our large American towns. Wm. J.H. Hough, fellow in architecture of the American Academy in Rome, has commandeered the local fire apparatus and is measuring mouldings on the Bernini colonnade in front of St. Peter's in Rome." American Academy in Rome Papers.

William J.H. Hough and Gorham Stevens measuring the Column of Trajan, 1917. American Academy in Rome Papers.

Students Philip T. Schutze, William J.H. Hough, and [Wilton?] measuring the capital of the Column of Trajan, 1917. American Academy in Rome Papers.

"When one of our native sons and an embryo architect desires to become thoroughly familiar with the precise size of a given detail on an old world monument, he generaly [sic] *goes after it in truly American fashion. Raymond Kennedy, fellow in architecture of the American Academy in Rome, as a human six foot rule, indicates the scale of the soffited dome of the Pantheon in Rome.*" American Academy in Rome Papers.

"In Rome, a man that supplies ladders for any and all occasions, even for buglary [sic]*, calls himself by the momentous title of aerial artist, but to our mind he has nothing on his patron, who, in this case, happens to be one Joe H. McDonnell on a McKim Scholarship in architecture and a visiting student of the American Academy in Rome who is measuring a detail that is inaccessable* [sic] *in any other way, on the Pandolfini Palace in Florence."*
American Academy in Rome Papers.

The American Academy in Rome's three new studios from the North, 1909. American Academy in Rome Papers.

AUGUST FLORIAN JACCACI (1856-1930)
French-American editor, Washington, D.C.

Material relating to Italian Renaissance critic and historian Bernard Berenson, 1896 and undated, including a letter to Jaccaci in which Berenson proposes articles he wants to write for a potential book and suggests photographs for reproduction, March 4, 1896; 1 postcard from Berenson thanking publishers Merrill and Baker for a photograph of a Botticelli; 1 letter from Berenson's brother to Jaccaci supplying Bernard's address and future plans, June 30 (no year). Also included are 2 lists of works by Italian painters, 1 with Berenson's comments. Microfilm roll D 118, frames 749-771.

THOMAS MORAN (1837-1926)
Landscape painter, New York, N.Y.

Two letters to Moses Tanenbaum, April 7, 1896, and undated. Moran invites Tanenbaum to visit his studio to see *Venice at Sunset*, which Moran is painting for him, 1896. In the other letter, Moran writes that he has made some minor changes in the painting and asks Tanenbaum again to come see them. Microfilm roll 97, frames 10, 51.

JOHN FERGUSON WEIR (1841-1926)
Sculptor, painter, Rome, Italy

Three sketchbooks of landscapes and figures in Italy, Switzerland, Holland, and France, 1896-1902. The sketches are done in watercolor, pencil, and ink wash. Microfilm roll 949, frames 750-834. Originals privately owned.

HARRY SIDDONS MOWBRAY (1858-1928)
Secretary and acting director, American Academy, Rome, Italy

Three diaries kept by Mowbray's wife, Helen, 1896 and 1902-1904. The first covers trips to Naples, Capri, Rome, Florence, Venice, and other Italian cities, May 16-September 19, 1896. In the second and third diaries, December 1902-February 1904, Mrs. Mowbray writes often about her husband's work on the Pinturicchio murals and his decision to assume the directorship of the American Academy in Rome, his friendly exchange of criticisms with Elihu Vedder, the planning and celebration of the 1904 exhibition and dinner, the unpopularity of Samuel Abbott and Ambassador Meyer and their wives, and the visit of King Edward VII to Rome. Academy students mentioned include Charles Keck and Andrew T. Schwartz, "who are poorly lodged and have no privileges whatever of the Academy," [Will Howe] Foote, [William H.] Hyde, and Franklin Simmons. Also included is a 5-pp. illustrated fairy tale inscribed "For George, Siena, 1902," probably referring to the Mowbray's son. Microfilm roll 2895.

Typescript of his autobiography, including accounts of his time spent in Rome, 1902-1904. Mowbray describes preparing decorations for the J.P. Morgan University Club Library from Pinturicchio's murals in the Borgia apartments and writes at length about problems at the Academy, its poor reputation, and the exhibition of 1904. Microfilm roll 1899, frames 137-179, 257-270.

Papers relating to his position as secretary and acting director of the American Academy in Rome, 1903-1904 (ca. 150 items). Material regarding the incorporation of the Academy includes a copy of a House of Representatives bill, January 1, 1904. Included are ca. 30 letters pertaining to Samuel Abbott's resignation as director of the Academy, Mowbray's appointment, alumni activities, future directors, and renewal of the lease on the Villa Aurora. Correspondents include Samuel Abbott, Theodore N.Ely, W.M. Kendall, C.G. La Farge, Joseph Cozza Luzi, Cameron Mark, Angelo di Matti, Charles McKim, Francis Davis Millet, Mowbray, E. Wood Perry, Alessandro Rocchi, Augustus Saint-Gaudens, and Gorham Phillips Stevens (frames 40-154, 233). A 1904 scrapbook contains memorabilia from a dinner reception for an exhibition opening at the Villa Aurora on January 11, 1904. It also includes guest lists, newspaper clippings, a 3-pp. handwritten speech, 2 photographs of the king and queen of Italy, and correspondence with invited state officials and artistic luminaries such as Samuel Abbott, Carlo Fiorilli, Eugene Guillaume, Robert Lovell, G.B.H. Meyer, Eliot Norton, Attilio Porizi, Luigi Rava, Franklin Simmons, Enrico Stelluti Stala, and Elihu Vedder (frames 1237-1302). Microfilm rolls 1898-1902.

JULIUS ROLSHOVEN (1858-1930)
American painter, Florence, Italy

Fifteen letters and postcards from him in Venice, Florence, Assisi, and Milan to his parents in Germany, 1899-1909. Included are envelopes and 1 letter from Edwin Denby in Venice describing his trip through Italy, June 2, 1911. Also included is Rolshoven's paint box. Not microfilmed.

WILLIAM STANLEY HASELTINE (1835-1900)
American painter, Rome, Italy

Correspondence includes 9 letters to Ellie Haseltine from friends who offer their sympathy at the time of her husband's death and who share fond reminiscences of the days they spent with the Haseltines in Rome, February 1900 and undated. One condolence is from William Draper, the American ambassador to Rome, lamenting the loss that the American colony there suffers in Haseltine's death. In addition, there are 2 typescript replies from friends of Haseltine to whom his daughter Helen wrote seeking recollections of her father. These letters stress his achievements as an artist and refer to sketches and paintings he made while in Italy. Also included are 5 personal letters from Haseltine to his wife, Ellie, written while he was traveling. The printed material includes an account of a visit to Haseltine's studio that appeared in the *Boston Standard* during the winter of 1895-1896. Microfilm roll D 295, frames 444-490. Originals in the Pennsylvania Academy of the Fine Arts, Philadelphia, Pa.

BARRY FAULKNER (1881-1966)
American painter, Rome and Florence, Italy

Papers relating to his travel and study at the American Academy in Rome and in Italy with George de Forest Brush, and his uncle, Abbott Handerson Thayer, 1900-1923 (ca. 30 items). Eighteen letters from Faulkner to his parents describe his travel and study with Thayer through Naples, Capri, Florence, Rome, Sardinia, and Venice, December 1900-May 1901. Faulkner describes how Thayer encouraged him to make studies of nudes and writes in detail about his native Italian models and the sketches he creates. He discusses the exhibition of one of Thayer's paintings in Venice and mentions visiting Elihu Vedder in Florence. Included are 6 typed and several fragments of letters from Faulkner in Rome and Florence to his friend Witter ("Hal") Bynner, in which he mentions a surprise visit from Brush, 1907; and 1 letter from Faulkner's aunt Emma Thayer to his parents, December 30, 1900. In addition, there is a copy of Faulkner's writings on Brush, describing Florence and Rome; a sketchbook containing scenes of Italy, labeled by town; and 3 diaries, describing works of art and towns including Padua, Perugia, Ravenna, and Rome, 1923 and undated. Not microfilmed.

WILLIAM ROBERT PEARMAIN (1888-1912)
American painter, Florence, Italy

Papers, including correspondence, a diary, biographical material, excerpts of writings, photographs, and miscellaneous printed material documenting his personal life and career, 1900-1945 (ca. 200 items). The correspondence includes ca. 80 letters from Pearmain while a student in Paris and at the Milton Academy to his parents in Boston, 1900-1908 and undated. In addition, there are 31 letters written between Pearmain and his future wife Nancy [Douglas Bowditch] while he studied painting with Nancy's father, George de Forest Brush, in Florence, 1906-1912 (ca. 125 pp.). The letters detail Pearmain's day-to-day activities, his future plans, and his emotional state to his family; there is almost no mention, however, of his progress in painting. There are also ca. 15 letters to Pearmain from his family offering family news and encouragement in his continued studies and travels, 1903-1912 and undated. Also included are 4 letters of condolence to Nancy Bowditch, 1912, as well as 3 letters from Bowditch to her daughters, 1942-1945. Pearmain's diary (91 pp.), which he kept while he lived in Florence, May-November 1907, records information about his models, studio, daily routines, and attempts to draw and paint. He also mentions a trip to the beach and an extended trip to Paris during October. Not microfilmed.

CHARLES KECK (1875-1951)
American sculptor, Rome, Italy

Twelve photographs of Keck's sculpture taken while he was a Rinehart scholar at the American Academy in Rome, 1901-1905. In addition, there are 2 photographs of Keck's studio arranged for an exhibition; 1 photograph of Keck with a group of Italian friends, May 1901; and 1 photograph of Keck with Harrison, a singer, and architect Andrew T.

Schwartz, all of whom were probably fellow students in Rome. Microfilm roll 441, frames 152-181.

ALLEN PHILBRICK (1879-1964)
Painter, Chicago, Ill.

Six letters to his future wife Edith Kellogg, 1904-1905, describing his travels and his progress painting landscapes and portraits in Rome, Capri, and Venice, Italy. Also included is 1 letter written to his mother while he was in Rome. Microfilm roll 4476, between frames 369 and 454.

BERTHA BECKWITH (Mrs. J. Carroll Beckwith) (1852-1917)
Artist's wife, Italy

Diary, 1904, partly kept in Italy where she was on a honeymoon trip with her husband, J. Carroll Beckwith. She writes of her husband's painting in the gardens of the Marquesa Natta in Orla, the food, lodgings, scenery, etc. In Venice she mentions meeting [William Gedney] Bunce and John Singer Sargent and of socializing with the Faulkners, Hastings, and Vails. They also visited Milan, Genoa, and Naples. Microfilm roll 1418.

GUSTAVO FRIZONNI (1840-1919)
Art historian, Milan, Italy

Sixteen letters of negotiation between him in Milan and Carl Snyder of Merrill and Baker Publishers in London for essays he is writing as part of the proposed book, "Notable Pictures in American Private Collections" (never published), to be edited by John La Farge and August F. Jaccaci, January-September 1904. They discuss the attribution of paintings, many in the [Isabella Stewart] Gardner Collection, payment for the essays, and suggestions for essays in later volumes (in English, French, and Italian). Microfilm roll D 119, frames 689-716.

GEORGE W. BRECK (1863-1920)
Mural painter, New York, N.Y.

Letter to Horace T. Carpenter of New York, N.Y., March 15, 1904. Breck writes that he is sorry to have missed Carpenter's visit and invites him back for a talk about Italy. Microfilm roll P 10, frame 311. Original in the Philadelphia Museum of Art, Philadelphia, Pa.

CHARLES CARYL COLEMAN (1840-1928)
American landscape painter, Capri, Italy

Five telegrams and 2 letters to his colleagues at *Century Magazine*, 1906-1912. Coleman reports he has received a permit to draw at Pompeii, offers his drawings of Mount Vesuvius to the magazine, and writes that he is making arrangements to interview Professor Matteucci. Matteucci responds by telegram saying he cannot do an article for *Century Magazine* as there is not enough time. Coleman writes to Johnson saying that if Johnson writes an article about Vesuvius, he will illustrate it. He writes that he asked Frank A. Perret, assistant at the Royal Observatorio Vesuviano, to sell some of his photographs of Vesuvius to American publications and that Professor Malladia accepted *Century Magazine*'s request for exclusive rights to his accounts of his explorations at Pompeii. Coleman also asks for the return of his sketches that were not accepted for the Christmas issue. Microfilm roll N 6, frames 1016-1034. Originals in the New York Public Library, New York, N.Y.

Newspaper clippings and photographs relating to Mount Vesuvius and Coleman's work in Italy (ca. 13 items). Included are 4 pp. of an article by William P. Andrews titled "Vesuvius in Fury: Causes and Characteristics of the Great Eruption of April 1906," published by *Century Magazine*, 1906, with a photograph of Coleman, Professor Matteucci, and Frank A. Perret on the terrace of the observatory at Pompeii, and 3 illustrations by Coleman of Mount Vesuvius erupting. There is 1 photograph of Coleman in his studio in Capri, Italy, wearing the costume of a Venetian senator, and 1 photograph of a painting of the interior of a building in Capri. An article from the *New York Herald* announces the exhibition of Coleman's pastels of Vesuvius in New York, N.Y., and notes that Coleman records the time of day and date each picture is made, December 23, 1906. Included also are 6 photographs of his paintings and 4 clippings about exhibitions of Coleman's work in New York, N.Y., and Boston, Mass., 1906-1915. Microfilm roll N 99, frames 119-129. Originals in the New York Public Library, New York, N.Y.

CHARLES HOFFBAUER (1875-1957)
American painter, Italy, Greece, and Egypt

Accounts of his travels in Italy, Greece, and Egypt, 1907-1909 (25 pp.). Most are written in French. One 9-pp. account describes Naples, undated. Not microfilmed.

ANTONIO SALEMME (b. 1892)
Italian painter, sculptor, United States and Italy

Extensive weekly correspondence from the United States and Italy with Miss Osgood, 1907-1922, and 49 letters from Augustus and Caroline Read, 1912-1917. Included also are 65 letters from various friends and museum and patron associations written upon his return from World War I; photographs of the artist and his paintings and sculptures; and a scrapbook kept from 1930 to 1965. Matters discussed in correspondence with Miss Osgood concern Salemme's studies as a child in the United States, his allowance used to study art and to buy materials, his studies as an artist in Rome before World War I, life as a soldier on the Italian front and loss of his boyhood innocence, his life in postwar Italy as an ambulance driver for the Red Cross, and finally his return to the

United States and new energy for painting and sculpting. Correspondence with Augustus and Caroline Read largely concerns finances. Their support of Salemme enables him to travel to Italy and to live in Rome before the war. During the war, correspondence with the Reads concerns Salemme's safety, the death of Augustus Read, and the death of Salemme's father. Among other printed materials upon his return to the United States are commissions, membership in the Architectural League of New York, appointment to the John Simon Guggenheim Memorial Foundation Fellowship, and letters from various philosophical and religious organizations regarding his statue of Swami Brahmananda. Microfilm rolls D 252-253.

WALTER PACH (1883-1958)
American artist, Florence, Italy

Materials written in Italian relating to his stay in Florence, October 5, 1907-February 1912 (7 items). Included is a letter to Pach from the provincial manager of the Royal House in Florence regarding the execution of a copy of the portrait of Catherine de Medici, October 5, 1907; a letter from Margherita Innocenti in which she sends Christmas wishes and mentions seeing a mutual friend Albert, December 22, 1911; a letter of welcome from Margherita to friends of Pach who are coming to stay with her in Florence, February 9, 1912; a calling card from Pietro Brunelleschi to Pach accepting an invitation; 2 postcards to Pach from Carlo [last name unknown] and Ariella Brunelleschi, daughter of Pietro. In addition there is 1 postcard to Mr. Gualtiero from Conforta V [?], undated. Microfilm roll 4216, frames 771-772, and roll 4217, frames 46-54.

FREDERICK GARRISON HALL (1878-1946)
American painter, Italy

Sketchbook with diary entries kept while traveling between Milan and Rome, August 31-October 16, 1908 (27 pp.). Hall describes his sight-seeing through all the major cities in Italy, despite recurring references to his poor health. He keeps an itemized list of his expenditures next to each entry, recording tips, food, hotels, postal fees, admission fees, art materials, transportation costs, etc. In Milan, he discusses his favorite paintings and artists in the museum and describes the interior of the cathedral. In Venice, he describes the Accademia, the Cà d'Oro, and the Ducal Palace, which he saw while working on sketches and a portrait. In Florence, he lists the paintings found in many of the churches. Upon his arrival in Rome, he writes that the ceiling of the Sistine Chapel is "beyond praise." Microfilm roll 1032, frames 806-1076.

PAUL MANSHIP (1885-1966)
Sculptor, New York, N.Y.

Papers relating to his association with the American Academy in Rome as a student, 1909-1912, and as trustee and president of the Alumni Association, 1941. Included is a photograph of Manship in his Rome studio, 1909, and a postcard from Rome to his cousin Sevilla Stees (frames 321-22). Printed material includes the transcript of a radio interview for the Metropolitan Museum of Art with Lucretia Osborn on WNYC, New York, during which Manship discusses his student years in Rome, June 4, 1941; an issue of *Art and Archeology* featuring Manship's article "The Sculptor at the American Academy," February 1925; 2 typed adaptations of the same article and a published version, "The American Academy in Rome: A Community of Artists," *Legion of Honor Magazine*, January 1938; and a handwritten transcript of a lecture to the Congress on Art, League of Nations, in Venice, in which Manship contrasts issues of patronage, commercialism, art education, and craftsmanship of the Renaissance and modern times, July 1934 (frames 385-389, 488-501, 615-620, 650-680). Microfilm roll NY 59-15.

Correspondence among Manship, family, and professional associates. A letter to his aunt, Virginia Stees, announces that he has won the Prix de Rome, July 19, 1909; a letter from Bernard Berenson concerns the William Church Osborn memorial gates at the Bearz bronze foundry, February 26, 1953; and a letter from Henry Kreis affirms that he will sit on a jury to select new fellows for the American Academy in Rome, March 21, 1947. Included are 5 letters related to Manship's election to the Accademia Nazionale di San Luca, Rome, and a copy of "La Reale Insigne Accademia di San Luca," 1952-1953 (frames 270-275). Three letters among correspondents Frederick Hartt, Manship, and James Kellum Smith concern Academy fellowships, 1947. Ca. 10 letters to and from Giuseppe Massari, 1940-1947, concern wartime supplies and Massari's visit to the United States (frames 454-456, 510-538). Microfilm roll NY 59-16.

ABEL G. WARSHAWSKY (1883-1962)
American painter, Italy

Typescript of his autobiography, which includes an account of his trip to Italy in 1909 with Samuel Halpert. Warshawsky describes their activities in each city they visit; writes about where and what he sketches, including San Giorgio in Venice, a view from his window in Naples, and the Duomo in Siena; and discusses the importance of color in painting, the work of Renaissance artist Giotto, and a John Singer Sargent painting in the piazza of Saint Mark's. He mentions a party with Barry Faulkner and Ivan Olinsky at the American Academy in Rome. A different version of the autobiography, ending in the mid-1920s, was published as *The Memories of an American Impressionist*, ed. Ben L. Bassham (Kent, Ohio: Kent State University Press, 1980).

ELSIE SPEICHER (Mrs. Eugene Edward Speicher)
Artist's wife, Woodstock, N.Y.

Two diaries kept during her travels with her husband in Europe, 1910-1926. In 1910 she describes a tour of England, Belgium, Holland, France, Germany, Italy, and Spain (ca. 186 pp.). The 1926 diary, written on the back of picture postcards of paintings, buildings, panoramic views of cities, and people wearing regional costumes, records a 1926 trip to France, Italy, England, Germany, Czechoslovakia, and Austria (176 items). In both diaries, she describes shopping trips, paintings, impressions of cities and hotels, and she occasionally refers to her husband's painting. Microfilm roll D 168, frames 444-802, 803-915.

Undated letter from Eugene Speicher to Robert Laurent. Speicher writes that he would like to spend a year in Rome under the auspices of the American Academy in Rome. Microfilm roll N68-3, frame 71.

MAURICE B. PRENDERGAST (1858-1924)
American painter, Venice, Italy
Letter to Mrs. Oliver Williams in Weston, Mass., December 18, 1911. Prendergast writes that he will be in Rome by the end of January and that he has not done much sketching because he was ill and had an operation. Microfilm roll 917, frames 219-221.

JOHN SINGER SARGENT (1856-1925)
American painter, London, England

One article, "Scopre a Carrara Tre Disegni Inediti di John Sargent," by "Spectator" in the Italian magazine *Noi e il Mondo*, about 3 unpublished drawings by Sargent, 1912. Microfilm roll D 177, frames 214-216.

WILLIAM MERRITT CHASE (1844-1916)
American painter, Venice, Italy

Ca. 15 letters to Mrs. Chase from Venice, where Chase was hosting summer art classes, July-August 1913. Chase writes of his search for a studio; the progress of his students; and painting scenes of fish markets and interiors from his balcony and in front of his class. He expresses his love for his wife and for his family and encourages her to take up painting. He describes meetings with Miss Ciardi, Mr. and Mrs. Robert de Forest, Madame Fortuny, and the Rolshovens and says he plans to visit the Doges Palace and the Tintorettos in the Scuola Saint Rocco. Microfilm roll N 69-137, frames 666-694.

DANIEL FELLOWS PLATT (1873-1938)
Collector, author, Englewood, N.J.

Papers, including ca. 20 letters from Italian Renaissance critics and historians Bernard and Mary Berenson, 1914-1963. Writing from their home, I Tatti, near Florence, the Berensons request photographs of Florentine drawings and other Italian works from Platt's collection, provide an introductory letter for Platt to the Parisian dealer Duveen, and thank Platt for sending them photographs and a catalog of the Frank Lusk Babbott Collection. Also included is a letter from Jesse Benedict Carter, the director of the American Academy in Rome, who introduces the Academy's librarian, Mr. S.B. Lathrop, and requests that he be permitted to view Platt's collection, August 2, 1913; 3 letters from Giacomo de Nicola, director of the Museo Nazionale, Florence, 1922;

and 2 letters from Umberto Gholi, director of the Galleria Nazionale dell' Umbria, Perugia, 1921. Also included are newspaper articles that dispute the authenticity of the works in Platt's collection. Microfilm roll D 316, frames 15-48.

ALDRO THOMPSON HIBBARD (1886-1972)
American painter, Italy

Diary of a European trip, including daily entries made during a tour of Italy, March 29-August 31, 1914. Hibbard visits Rome, Pisa, and Naples and spends several weeks in Capri, Venice, and Chioggia. He writes about the daily activities of villagers, exploring Capri with native islanders, enjoying the company of other artists in Venice, and the landscapes and the subjects he paints and sketches. He describes developments as World War I begins and his arrest in Venice as a spy. Microfilm roll 373, frames 192-244.

MARTIN BIRNBAUM (1878-1970)
American art dealer, writer, New York, N.Y.

Photograph of Martin Birnbaum, Edward Bruce, Alfred Potterton, Leo Stein, and Maurice Sterne at Anticoli Corrado, near Rome, ca. 1915. Microfilm roll 1027, frame 812.

Twelve letters from friends and artists in Italy. In 6 letters from Rome, painter Maurice Sterne writes that his school is doing well, asks if Birnbaum would be interested in some sculptures by a German working in Rome, and describes a sculpture of a head of the Buddha that he owns and wants to sell, January 10, 1924-December 20, 1926. He also keeps Birnbaum informed of his projects and writes that he hopes to produce some first-class works. A letter from New York, N.Y., Emma S. Bellows, widow of George Wesley Bellows, includes a diagram for the arrangement of her late husband's pictures at the [International Art Exhibition], Venice, April 12, 1932. She says she may go to Venice for the exhibition and that American art will be given the attention it deserves because Birnbaum is the master of ceremonies. In 5 letters from Florence, Lina Cavaliere writes of shopping and sight-seeing trips and financial matters, December 15, 1938, and undated. She says she does not like living alone and would like to bring a friend or relative to Italy to live with her if she could afford it. In another letter, she says she has leased her house and is moving to Los Angeles but is staying in the pensione in Florence for the time being. Microfilm roll 108, frame numbers illegible.

ALLYN COX (1896-1982)
American painter, New York, N.Y.

Letters to his family when he was a fellow at the American Academy in Rome, 1916-1922. In his letters of 1916-1917, Cox describes his studio at the Academy and sight-seeing trips around Rome and other Italian cities. He says he plans to submit his work to exhibitions, traces the progress of his painting, and describes his fellow students, Cowles, a painter, and architects Hough and Shutze. Cox often expresses exasperation with the Academy ("an infinitesimal world of petty things," frame 119) and its directors Gorham Phillips Stevens and Dr. Carter. Cox critiques the frescoes of Urbino and Florence and comments on Baroque and Florentine architecture and various works of art by Botticelli, Caravaggio, Giotto, Perugino, Raphael, and Andrea del Sarto. Cox describes American society in Rome and his encounters with various foreigners, including British Academy lecturer Mrs. Arthur, the Conte Dottore Umberto Guoli, the Count Primoli, and author Geoffrey Scott. After Scott and art historian Bernard Berenson review Cox's painting, Cox writes that the latter "begins gently to take you apart, tenderly and somewhat sadly tearing you limb from limb, and slowly, carefully, pulverizing the remains" (frame 1920). Ca. 20 letters beginning in May 1918 trace Cox's work with the American Red Cross as a supervisor of Italian embroidery workshops in Rimini and Venice during World War I. Microfilm roll N 69-9.

Two letters from Mary and Bernard Berenson to Cox's father, Kenyon Cox, discussing Allyn's work at the American Academy in Rome and his visits to their home, I Tatti, near Florence, June 29 and August 31, 1917. Ca. 20 letters from the Berensons to Allyn Cox invite Cox to visit and study with them and offer criticism and encouragement for his painting, 1917-1920. Microfilm roll N 69-10.

Papers concerning his tenure in New York as a member of the board of trustees and the committee on fine arts of the American Academy in Rome, 1960-1963. This material includes letters and director's reports from Michael Rapuano, president of the American Academy in Rome, and Mary T. Williams, executive secretary. Rapuano describes Academy exhibitions, new fellows, visitors, fund-raising activities, and special events. Microfilm roll N 69-10, frames 197-295.

ONORIO RUOTOLO (1888-1966)
Italian sculptor, New York, N.Y.

Scrapbooks, photographs, and writings by Ruotolo and Augusto Bellanca, 1917-1958. Included are a poem and a book of poetry by Ruotolo, a biography of Augusto Bellanca, a book of Bellanca's poetry, and a manuscript by A. Giovannitti, "Quando Canta Il Gallo." The 26 photographs include images of Ruotolo, his work, and the Amalgamated Clothing Workers of America conventions. Only the 2 scrapbooks have been microfilmed. Microfilm roll 2526.

KAY (KATHERINE LINN) SAGE (1898-1963)
American painter, Rome and Rapallo, Italy

Ca. 7 photographs, 1925 and 1930, and 25 letters, undated and 1919-1922, from Sage in Rome to her father, Henry Manning Sage, and stepmother and half-sister, both named Cornelia. In the photographs, Sage is depicted on the day of her marriage to Prince Ranieri di San Faustino in Venice and at the Palazzo Rospigliosi in Rome. She illustrates several of her letters with pencil drawings and writes at length about her studies in Rome at the British and French academies and her private lessons with

Battaglia, Onorato Carlandi, and Carosi. She describes her studio on Via Margutta and discusses sketching and painting in the Roman Forum, at Hadrian's Villa, and in the countryside. She also describes meeting various members of Italian and American society, including Sinclair Lewis, and reports on a fascist uprising in 1922, at which Mussolini appeared. Microfilm roll 2886, frames 56ff., and roll 2888, frames 495ff.

Edited typescript of her 1955 autobiography, "China Eggs," in which she writes about her life until ca. 1935 (165 pp.). Sage describes her childhood, her parents' divorce, her mother's morphine addiction, her marriage to and subsequent divorce from Prince Ranieri di San Faustino, her travels in Italy and Spain, and other events in her personal life. Included is an account of her life in Rome, where she trained as a painter at the Scuola Libera delle Belle Arte and with Italian landscape artist Onorato Carlandi. She also writes about her friendship with Ezra Pound, whom she met while living in Rapallo (133 pp.). Microfilm roll 685. Restricted access. Prior permission required.

MARGERY RYERSON (b. 1886)
Painter, engraver, teacher, writer, New York, N.Y.

Letter from H[enry] M. Rosenberg in Halifax, Nova Scotia, August 17, 1920. He writes of engraver Otto Henry Bacher's pleasant personality and of Whistler's influence on Bacher's work. Rosenberg notes that Bacher went to Venice in 1879-1880 and that one of Bacher's friends in New York City still has some of the plates he did in Venice. He mentions it is unfortunate that diary notes from Bacher's time in Venice are probably lost and asks Ryerson to send him a copy of her article about Bacher. Microfilm roll 962, frames 2-4.

VACLAV VYTLACIL (1892-1984)
American painter, France and Italy

Letters, 1 diary, and 1 list of works relating to Vytlacil's painting and years spent in France and Italy (27 items). Included are ca. 25 letters to Elizabeth Foster (later his wife) while traveling in France, Czechoslovakia, Germany, and Italy, 1920-1929. He writes of his art studies and repeatedly asks her to visit him. In the diary kept when they lived in Paris, France, and Positano and Capri, Italy, Elizabeth Foster Vytlacil writes about domestic issues, her husband's work, their relationship, current economic and political conditions, and the fast-paced social life of some of their American acquaintances, 1931-1940 (ca. 460 pp.). There is also a list of Vytlacil's paintings and their buyers, completed in 1966. Microfilm roll D 295, frames 1-326. Originals privately owned.

Letter to Morris Kantor, February 5, 1956. Vytlacil writes of travels with his wife in Italy and Spain and comments that Positano has been spoiled and is now "honky-tonk." Microfilm roll D 114, frames 315-316.

MARSDEN HARTLEY (1877-1943)
American painter, Venice, Italy

Eleven letters to Mathilde Rice in Paris, May 11, 1922-February 2, 1926, postmarked 1927, and undated from Berlin, Venice, and Aix-en-Provence. In 4 letters from Venice, Hartley writes that he is annoyed with the gossiping, affected British who treat Venice like a suburb of London. He writes of patrons who "want their money worshipped" and are disappointed when they see that his studio is not all "charm and romance." He says he is sorry Mathilde has been ill and that she should come to Venice with her mother to rest before going to the United States. He writes of mutual friends, his friend Eugene O'Neill, and his acquaintance with the daughter of a well-known French artist. Microfilm roll 130, frames 55-102.

RENE GIMPEL (1881-1945)
Art dealer, Paris, France

Two letters from Italian Renaissance critic and historian Bernard Berenson, December 24, 1923, and November 9, 1924. The first wishes Gimpel a happy new year and requests that he send Berenson's share of profits from a sale. The second reviews their arrangement whereby Berenson would receive a quarter of all profits collected on sales that he suggests. Berenson proposes possible attributions for a painting and advises caution in buying. Microfilm roll 918.

ALLEN TOWNSEND TERRELL (b. 1897)
American painter, architect, Italy

Letters written every other day to his parents while he was traveling through Italy and living in Rome, September 26, 1924-May 4, 1925 (620 pp.). Included is an index outlining the lengthy, 6-8 pp. letters recording every place he visited. Terrell writes in September about his plans to travel to Italy with 2 classmates, William Foster and a woman named Helen, upon finishing his studies at Fontainebleau. Before settling in Rome for 7 months, he and his companions travel to Bologna, Capri, Florence, Lake Como, Milan, Naples, Venice, and Verona. He relates amusing anecdotes about missing trains and arguing with his companions and with a *pensione* owner. He also describes the rise of the facist regime while he lived in Rome and the resulting military presence. Not microfilmed.

ALPHEUS HYATT MAYOR (1901-1980)
Curator of prints, Museum of Modern Art, New York, N.Y.

Diary kept during a visit to Florence, December 1924-January 1925. Mayor writes about the art and architecture he sees in museums and churches, including the Accademia, the Bargello, the Museo Archeologico, the Opera del Duomo, Palazzo Vecchio, the Pitti Palace, San Lorenzo, Santa Croce, Santa Maria, Santo Spirito, and the Uffizi Gallery. He describes visits and outings with American and Italian friends including the families of Harold Acton and Teddy Spencer, the Stonehills, Count Fabbri, and his sister Countess Gundolfi Fabbri. Posing as a millionaire, Mayor visits the gallery of Volterra and assesses the authenticity of several works. He describes in detail his visit with Bernard and Mary Berenson at their home, I Tatti, near Florence, January 5, 1925. Mayor records Berenson's comments about contemporary scholarship, the merits of Italian over Flemish painting, and the importance of teaching while one is still a student. On January 10-11, Mayor spends the weekend with the Berensons. He describes their luncheon with Professor Kontovowicz of the University of Freiburg. He also describes the Tuscany landscape and repeats many of Berenson's insights about art history and suggestions for Mayor's career. Microfilm roll 2322, frames 745-758.

ISE GROPIUS (Mrs. Walter Gropius) (1897-1983)
German architect's wife, Italy

English translation of her diary recording travels to southern Italy with her husband, Walter Gropius, February 2-March 4, 1925 (8 pp.). Towns to which they travel include Genoa, Naples, Pompeii, the island of Procida, and Pozzuoli. She describes the beauty of Italy and the cultural differences between Germans and Italians. Microfilm roll 2393, frames 312-321.

EDWARD BRUCE (1879-1943)
American painter, Venice, Italy

Letter to Martin Birnbaum from Venice, October 25, 1925. Bruce hopes that a prospective exhibition of Maurice Sterne's work will be held at Birnbaum's gallery and comments on Birnbaum's Topi drawings. Microfilm roll 108, frames 877-883. Original in the Martin Birnbaum papers.

ITALY AMERICA SOCIETY
New York, N.Y.

Invitation, pamphlet, and catalog for a 1926 art exhibition titled "Black and White," sponsored by the Italy America Society. In the pamphlet, the exhibition is described as the first exhibition in the United States of works by living Italian artists. "Black and White" is also listed as a traveling exhibition to "visit the principal cities in the United States." Microfilm roll N 118, frames 7-14. Originals in the New York Public Library, New York, N.Y.

GOTTARDO PIAZZONE (1872-1945)
Painter, California

Biographical information, letters and postcards, inventory of paintings, newspaper clippings, and photographs of the artist, his family, and some of his paintings, 1927-1969 (ca. 63 items). The biographical sketch mentions that he lived and exhibited his works in Rome for 1 year. Letters from friends and students to his daughter, Mireille Piazzoni Wood, tell their memories of her father and recall time spent in Rome in 1906, while the newspaper clippings include his obituary and notices of exhibitions of his work, 1945-1968. Microfilm roll 1902, frames 266-367.

ANNITA DELANO (1894-1979)
Painter, designer, teacher, Los Angeles, Calif.

Travel journal documenting her trip to Italy, with detailed accounts and sketches of Assisi, Capri, Florence, Palermo, Pompeii, Rome, and Venice, 1928-1929 (51 pp.). Delano's descriptions focus on ruins, mosaics, museums, frescoes, fountains, terrace gardens, and architectural structures. In Rome, she takes a day trip to Tivoli and to Hadrian's Villa, which she says was "the most interesting of all." In addition, there is an itemized list of hotel and travel expenses (4 pp.), miscellaneous receipts, and a list of sites to see in each city (19 pp.). Microfilm roll 2999, frames 1128-1407.

STEFANO CUSUMANO (1912-1975)
Italian-American painter, New York, N.Y.

Papers, 1929-1965 (235 items). Included are an artistic statement and autobiographical information describing his Italian heritage and his visit to Sicily to see his family's homeland (9 pp.); letters from Italy, 1939-1965, including 4 from Italian sculptor Carmelo Cappello; 5 from American painter Sidney Delevante, including a poem; and 15 others, including 1 from Esther Cecilia in Rome. In addition, there are notices of Cusumano's work, an English translation of a catalog, photographs, sketchbooks, teaching material, a scrapbook, exhibition catalogs, and miscellaneous printed material. Microfilm roll D 254, frames 934-1369.

Papers, 1937-1971 (1 ft.), including biographical material; letters from Samuel Adler, Sidney Delevante, Margaret Breuning, and others; poems, lectures, drafts of a book on structure and drawing, catalogs, photographs, and printed material. Microfilm rolls 296-297.

AUGUST MOSCA (b. 1909)
Italian-American painter, New York, N.Y.

Papers, 1930-1967 (ca. 200 items), including correspondence; photographs of Mosca and his work; sketches; a diary with entries made irregularly from January 4, 1965 to ca. November 1967; exhibition catalogs; clippings; and a handwritten draft of a speech on contemporary liturgical art. There are also papers concerning Joseph Stella, including letters from Stella, reproductions of Stella's paintings, sketches, and printed material. Microfilm roll 1576.

Papers relating to Joseph Stella, 1938-1944 (52 items), including letters and postcards from Stella; Mosca's reminiscences of Stella; Mosca's correspondence with M. Knoedler & Co. about Stella exhibitions; a typed prospectus for the Joseph Stella School of Art; and a Mosca exhibition catalog preface written by Stella. Microfilm roll N 70-7.

GEORGE BIDDLE (1885-1973)
American painter, Italy

Three letters in Italian, addressed to "Illustre Signore," from Nino Barbantini in Venice, ca. 1930s, 1 of which includes a note added by Marguerite Sarfatti. Barbantini's stationery reads, "Città di Venezia, Ispettorato delle Belle Arti." Microfilm roll P 17, frames 449-451. Originals in the Philadelphia Museum of Art, Philadelphia, Pa.

Typescript of a diary kept while traveling and working in Italy, October 14, 1951-September 20, 1952. While staying at the American Academy in Rome, Biddle writes about creating and producing lithographs with Roberto Bulla; making several trips, once with Mike Hammond, to visit and sketch George Santayana in the Calvary Hospital; attempting, unsuccessfully, to gain a commission for a mural from the Italian minister of fine arts; traveling with his wife, sculptor Helene Sardeau, and Marguerite Sarfatti down the Adriatic Coast to Taranto; and socializing with Roffredo Caetini, Ambassador [James Clement] Dunn, Lucas Foss, Isamu Noguchi, Isabel Roberts, and Lionello Venturi. Biddle also describes at length his visits to Bernard Berenson at I Tatti and Vallombroso, their conversations, and Berenson's visit to Biddle at Amalfi. He includes his impressions of the mosaics and frescoes he views at Arezzo, Florence, Ravenna, Rome, and other Italian towns. In addition there are 14 letters from Berenson to Biddle in which he discusses Mary McCarthy, Santayana, Gertrude and Leo Stein, Leo Steinberg, representational art, and both his and Biddle's writings, 1949-1957. Microfilm roll 3621, frames 402-433, 839-851.

GARI MELCHERS (1860-1932)
Painter, New York, N.Y.

Letter to the American ambassador to Italy, John W. Garrett, introducing his friend, Ehrich Kensett Rossiter, November 14, 1930. Melchers writes of Rossiter's upcoming trip to Rome and informs Garrett that Rossiter will visit the embassy in Rome. Microfilm roll D 33, frame 316.

BYRON THOMAS (1902-1978)
American painter, Italy

Journals kept while in Europe, 1930-1931, June-July 1960, and June-August 1962. In his 1930 journal, Thomas records the masterpieces and architecture he sees. In 1960, he travels with his son Richard and a young girl named Nini Chapman. While in Italy, he describes meeting with the Countess Brambein and Sir D'Arcy Osborne, the former minister of the Vatican. He also records meeting with Mr. Wadsworth, an American ambassador to the disarmament conference in Geneva. In 1962 he travels with his family to Europe. While in Italy, Thomas describes his stay in Spoleto during the Festival of Two Worlds, for which he contributes a painting to be used on the set of "Romantic Death" (frame 564). His diary includes an introduction written after his return to the United States. Microfilm roll 1417, frames 311-1326.

GIORGIO CAVALLON (1904-1989)
Italian painter, New York, N.Y.

Ca. 100 items documenting his career, 1931-1982. Included are 25 letters to him in Italian from Lonigo and Locara, Italy, September 1933-December 1954; 40 postcards from various points in Italy, 1931-1968; a 3-pp. biography and time line which lists Cavallon's exhibitions; a sketchbook from Italy, 1931; letters from Samuel Kootz regarding gallery business; 1 letter to Kootz from Milan regarding the sale of Cavallon's *Untitled GC.57*; a photograph of Cavallon's work; and photographs of him and others. Included also are letters from various American institutions and galleries regarding exhibitions, donations, and lectures. Microfilm rolls N68-60, N68-61.

DANIEL VARNEY THOMPSON, JR. (1902-1980)
Art historian, Boston, Mass., and London, England

Originals and typed copies of 81 letters from Bernard Berenson in Italy, 1933-1957. Berenson writes about family matters, travels, his research on Michelangelo, recent publications, the methodology of art history, and his concern over bequeathing his home, I Tatti, to Harvard University. He remarks on Thompson's theories and publications and encourages him to pursue jobs at the Courtauld Institute, Ireland's National Gallery, the Harvard Press, and the Walters Art Gallery. In addition, Berenson writes about mutual acquaintances, including Mrs. Alfred Barr, Kenneth Clark, Lewis Clark, W.G. Constable, Bella Greene, Paul Sachs, and Edith Wharton. Microfilm roll 888, frames 1-455.

HELEN GERARD
American children's author, translator, Florence, Italy

Two letters to [Leila] Mechlin, February 19, 1934, and April 26, 1935. Gerard writes of her daughter Paula's prints, frescoes, and writings about film and drama. She also explains that because of the [stock market] crash, the publisher has put her children's book about farm life in Tuscany on hold. She says she and her daughters may go to Paris to try to find work before returning to the United States. Microfilm roll P 10, frames 645-646. Originals in the Philadelphia Museum of Art, Philadelphia, Pa.

PAULA GERARD (b.1907)
American lithographer, fresco painter, film and drama critic, Florence, Italy

Letter to [Leila] Mechlin thanking her for her assistance in persuading Dr. Holland of the Library of Congress to accept some of her prints, February 20, 1934. She praises Mechlin's active participation in the advancement of the arts. With it is a French newspaper article about the Italian film director, Giovacchino Forzano, and his new film, *Campo di Maggio*, March 27, 1935. Microfilm roll P 10, frames 647. Originals in the Philadelphia Museum of Art, Philadelphia, Pa.

WILLIAM MILLIKEN (1889-1978)
Director, Cleveland Museum of Art, Cleveland, Ohio

Letters, a daybook, a passport, and other materials relating to his annual trips to Italy as museum director (9 items). Seven letters, 1934-1947, 4 of which are in Italian, include 1 from Gustavo Ballardini of the Faenza Museum of Ceramics, requesting a donation from the Cleveland Museum to repair damages caused by World War II; 1 from Ulrich Middeldorf, chair of the University of Chicago Art Department, regarding a donation to the Faenza Museum, September 30, 1946; and 1 from Professor Wart Arslan of Milan, acknowledging the receipt of a bulletin sent by Milliken, September 9, 1946. The letters in Italian are from Gicondo Momicchioli and Forsini. Microfilm roll 1276, frames 326-560.

STANLEY MUSCHAMP
Artist, Philadelphia, Pa.

Four letters to A. Margaretta Archambault, 1934-1946. Muschamp invites Archambault to his studio and to an anniversary party. He also mentions that he and his wife spent the summer of 1936 in Italy. Microfilm roll P 27, frames 12-15. Originals in the Historical Society of Pennsylvania, Philadelphia, Pa.

EUGENE BERMAN (1899-1972)
American graphic artist, painter, designer, Rome, Italy

Papers, including correspondence, drawings, sketches, printed material, and photographs (loose and 1 album) and blank postcards of his works, all pertaining to his artistic career in Italy, 1937-1970 and undated (ca. 1,500 items). The correspondence includes 60 postcards from friends inviting him to parties and discussing travel plans, 1932-1957 and undated; 4 Christmas cards from Ernest E. Gottlieb, Juliet and Man Ray, and James and Eleanor Soby, 1950 and undated; and 1 letter in French from Berman to Leonid [?] in which he criticizes galleries that act as merchants and suggests vacation spots in Italy, August 3, 1970. Also included are 8 sketches and 3 drawings, all undated. The printed material includes 15 exhibition catalogs, 1962-1970 and undated, 4 of which are from galleries in Italy; 5 exhibition announcements, 1941-1970 and 1 guidebook, undated; 1 book of sketches titled "From the Roman Sketchbook," 1958; 1

guidebook from Vicenza; 1 album of Rembrandt's works; and 1 ballet program from the Royal Opera House, London, 1950. There are 2 newspaper articles and 6 newspaper clippings from *Le Figaro* concerning Leonid [?], 1975 and undated. Also included are 109 photographs of Berman's works, 1937-1967 and undated; 161 postcards of his works, 1937-1970 and undated; and 25 prints, 1947-1950 and undated. In addition, there are ca. 700 photographs of Italian art and architecture that Berman took while traveling in Italy, as well as ca. 200 negatives, 1932-1935 and undated, which are accompanied by ca. 800 blank postcards of similar subjects. Finally, 44 photographs record the costume and set designs which Berman created for a production of *Cosi Fan Tutte*, 1956. There is also 1 photograph album of Berman's works, 1942-1945. Not microfilmed.

Papers, including correspondence, photographs, and printed material documenting his artistic activities after settling in Rome in 1958 (ca. 200 items). Correspondence pertains to the publication of "The Graphic Works of Eugene Berman" (never published) and includes letters from Berman, the publisher Clarkson Potter, and Russell Lynes, who writes the foreword to the book, 1969-1972 (51 letters). They discuss expenses, format, and photographs. Also included are 9 photographs taken by Lynes of Berman in his studio and library in Rome and working on a painting, February 1969. Five contact sheets contain 131 prints, from which the photographs were made. The printed material includes press releases, a review of the book, and 6 exhibition catalogs and announcements of Berman's works, 1954-1969 and undated (71 pp.). The announcements are from galleries in Italy and the United States, among them the Larcada Gallery in New York, N.Y. Microfilm roll 494, frames 1158-1386.

Interview with Eugene Berman conducted by Paul Cummings as a part of the Oral History Program of the Archives of American Art, June-October 1972 (4 sound tape reels).

SOCIETY OF AMERICAN GRAPHIC ARTISTS (formerly Society of American Etchers), Brooklyn, N.Y.

Catalog of an exhibition of 100 works by American artists, sponsored by the Society at the Palazzo Antici-Mattei in Rome, June 1938 (ca. 50 pp.) Microfilm roll N 68-111, frames 291-315.

Papers relating to the Society of American Etchers' effort to mount an exhibition of graphic art to be shown at the Venice Biennale, March 1940-February 1941 (ca. 340 items). Included are letters from John Taylor Arms inviting artists to participate in the exhibit and their replies. Artists Peggy Bacon and Philip Evergood refused to contribute because of their aversion to fascism (microfilm roll N 68-110, frames 59, 77). In other letters Arms asks several artists if they objected to publicity about the purchase of their work by the king of Italy. Also included are the rules and regulations of the exhibit; expense records; correspondence with their Italian agent, Fabio Mauroner, about the early closing due to the war; lists of artists to be represented, with price, size, title, and medium of each work. Microfilm roll N 68-110, frames 49-198, and roll N 68-107, frames 235-299.

LUIGI LUCIONI (b. 1900)
Italian-American artist, Vermont and New York

Materials relating to his career (17 items). There are 9 letters from various admirers, 1940-1941; 3 catalogs of exhibitions in Vermont; and newspaper clippings announcing the awarding of a prize to his painting *John LaFarge*. Among the letters is 1 from the director of the Corcoran Gallery of Art, C. Powell Minnigerode, April 30, 1941, in which he presents the award of $200 for the popular prize; 1 from Blanche Pfuelzer offering to purchase *Vermont Splendor* for $1,000; 1 from Michael Cresci requesting to buy 1 of Lucioni's sketches, October 1941; and 1 from William K. Ruscoe, who requests that Lucioni donate a sketch for a proposed collection to be given to a small town in Connecticut. Included is a 23-p. catalog of an exhibition of Lucioni's paintings at the Shelburne Museum's Webb Gallery of American Art, June-August 1968. Microfilm roll 3134, frames 685-729.

MAX WEBER (1881-1961)
Painter, Long Island, N.Y.

Untitled address on the National Gallery of Art in Washington, D.C., in which he gives reasons why an artist would visit a museum and criticizes the Greco-Roman architecture as being too monumental and overshadowing the art, April 2, 1941 (6 pp.). Weber lists his favorite paintings at the National Gallery and writes that the Samuel H. Kress, Andrew W. Mellon, and Joseph E. Widener art collections will make the Gallery a viable force among museums. Microfilm roll N 69-112, frames 198-200.

ALEXANDER DOBKIN (1908-1975)
American painter, Italy
Sketchbooks, including ca. 90 sketches done in Italy, 1943-1966. Dobkin's subjects include landscapes and street scenes of Arezzo, Florence, Padua, Pisa, Positano, Rome, Siena, and Venice. Also included are numerous postcards, photographs, writings, stamps, and a sketch of Raphael Soyer in Florence, July 11, 1959. Microfilm rolls N 68-99, N 68-100, N 69-2.

ROSE FRIED GALLERY
New York, N.Y.

Files on artists, including Italians Giorgio de Chirico, Sergio Dangelo, and Piero Dorazio, and Futurist artists Giacoma Balla and Gino Severini, 1945-1971. The files include (microfilm roll 2202): for de Chirico, correspondence and photographs regarding his work (11 items); for Dangelo, correspondence with the Schwarz Gallery in Milan, including a list of paintings and prices, ca. 1962; and for Dorazio, correspondence relating to sales of his and other Modernist works (ca. 80 letters, 1957). The file on Balla contains material relating to a 2-person exhibition of Balla and Severini in 1954, including correspondence among Fried, Balla, and his daughter Luce (11 letters);

insurance, shipping, and customs documents; 1 catalog; lists of titles and prices; and correspondence with museums and galleries (microfilm roll 2201). Included in the Severini file are 25 letters (Severini writes in French); 2 catalogs; ca. 20 photographs of his mosaics and early drawings; and miscellaneous papers (microfilm roll 2206). Microfilm rolls 2200-2209.

VIRGINIA ADMIRAL (b. 1915)
American painter, Venice, Italy

Correspondence and papers, ca. 1947-1978 (111 items), including a proposal for a play based on Doris Lessing's *The Four-Gated City*, 1977; legal and financial documents, undated (19 items); 5 exhibition catalogs, 1948; 19 exhibition announcements; 3 copies of a manuscript, 1969; demonstration notices from the Art Worker's Coalition; 4 newspaper clippings; and miscellaneous printed material (124 items). Fifty-one letters include 3 personal letters from Robert [Mapplethorpe] concerning their apartment building, 1974-1978; 1 letter from Mark Rothko requesting biographical information for an exhibition catalog to be written by Peggy Guggenheim, undated; and letters, Christmas cards, and invitations to openings from artists Nell Blaine, Charles Brega James, Joseph Kosuth, and others. Legal and financial documents include papers relating to property for sale in the British Virgin Islands and receipts from the sale of Admiral's paintings. The exhibition catalogs include 2 from "La Collezione Peggy Guggenheim," in Venice. The material from the Art Worker's Coalition includes 2 copies of *An Open Hearing*, a publication related to a protest against the Museum of Modern Art, 1969. The printed material includes a petition to the House of Representatives demanding Richard Nixon's impeachment, 1973; 2 books of poetry, 1 by Admiral's ex-husband Robert De Niro; 2 pamphlets; and a book titled *Artists in Metropolis*. Not microfilmed.

PEGGY GUGGENHEIM (1898-1979)
American art collector, Venice, Italy

Two letters to Clement Greenberg, December 2, 1947, and February 12, 1958. In the first letter, Guggenheim expresses her concern that her collection of paintings will be shown at the Biennale and asks Greenberg if the collection is an accurate representation of American avant-garde painters. She describes her attempts to buy a Venetian palace and convert it into a museum. In the second letter, she writes of Jackson Pollock's debt to her and complains that Lee Krasner does not give her credit for her help. She also refers to Pollock's death. Microfilm roll N 70-7, frames 472-473, 596. Restricted access. Use requires prior permission.

JULIAN LEVI (1900-1982)
American painter, New York, N.Y., and Rome, Italy

Correspondence relating mainly to Levi's association with the American Academy in Rome, 1948-1972 (71 items). Ca. 20 letters from the Academy request Levi's participation on the jury to elect new fellows for the Academy, January 1948-February 1970. Included are 2 lists of candidates selected to show their art to the Academy's jury, a receipt of Levi's autobiography given to the Academy, and an invitation from the Academy's director, Frank E. Brown, to spend the sabbatical year 1967-1968 in Rome as an artist in residence. Additional correspondence includes 18 letters from artist Gregorio Prestopino, September 1965-ca. 1972, and ca. 20 letters from various friends and institutions written to Levi in Rome, October 16, 1967-May 9, 1968. These correspondents include Allen Austill, Peter Blume, Edward Casacely, Korean painter Hei Myung Choi, Mrs. Stuart Davis, Robert Hale, Hilda Hunting, Eloise Spaeth, the Art Students' League of New York, the New School for Social Research, and the Pennsylvania Academy of the Fine Arts. Also included are ca. 13 letters to Levi following his departure from the Academy, including letters from instructors Lewis Cohen, Gregorio Prestopino, Jean Ribustini, and Michael Spafford, May 1968-March 1970. Microfilm rolls 483-485, frames 986ff.

ESTHER ROLICK (b. 1922)
American artist, teacher, Palermo, Italy

Forty-two undated photographs of people and architecture in Palermo. Not microfilmed.

AUGUST MOSCA (b. 1909)
Italian-American painter, Bronx, N.Y.

Papers, including correspondence and photographs pertaining to his artistic career, 1950-1969 and undated (ca. 110 items). Correspondence relates to the sale of his paintings and includes invitations to lectures and congratulations on the success of his exhibition (90 letters). There are letters from Nathan Cummins, Stefano Cusumano, Jessica Gasparo, Alfred Russell, Seymour Tubis, Roger Van Damme and the Harry Salpeter Gallery in New York, N.Y., which represented Mosca. Also included are 2 exhibition catalogs of Joseph Stella's works (1968), with whom Mosca studied, and 6 photographs of Mosca and his works. Microfilm roll N 69-112, frames 68-187.

LAWRENCE CALCAGNO (b. 1913)
Painter, New York, N.Y.

Three letters written to his family from Europe, 1951. Calcagno writes from Madrid, Florence, and Paris about family, friends, art, and the political and economic problems of postwar Europe. While traveling from Italy to France, he meets British poet Stephen Spender and gives him a drawing as a gift. Microfilm roll N 70/43.

FRANCES STILLMAN (Mrs. Ary Stillman)
American artist's wife, Europe

Diary documenting her travels to France, Italy, and Spain with her husband, painter Ary Stillman, May-November 1952 (105 pp.). Except during a visit to Nice, Frances Stillman wrote entries daily, documenting her experiences in the cities and villages of Europe and her impressions of museums, restaurants, and the people she and her husband meet. While in Paris, she describes an "at home" they attended at the studio of André Lhote. Ary Stillman was not impressed by Lhote's paintings, which he described as "reduced to formula with no emotion," and Stillman continued to defend his style of Abstract Expressionism despite the onslaught of criticism. In June, she writes of meeting Peggy Guggenheim during their stay in Venice and of visiting Guggenheim at her palace on the Grand Canal. Frances Stillman mentions looking at Guggenheim's art collection and especially liking the paintings by her ex-husband Max Ernst. In addition to Venice, she describes travels through Assisi, Florence, Rome, and Siena, but mentions that neither she nor her husband are particularly devoted to studying the Renaissance. While in Nice, she writes about visiting Henri Matisse's Chapelle du Rosaire, which she feels is his best work. In August, she and her husband befriend a Spanish painter, [?] Saponaro, while on the way to Barcelona. He guides them through the city and suggests that they visit the mountain village of Solsona because of their interest in Catalán painting and sculpture. There they meet the Spanish muralist Soler, with whom they discuss their mutual interest in the spiritual aspects of art. Soler recommends that they go to the cathedral museum in Gerona to see the Creation Tapestry and the Beatus manuscript. In September, she writes about how luxurious it feels to be back in Paris and about enrolling in conversation classes at the Alliance Française. She mentions the warm welcome from Monsieur and Madame Droze in Senlis, whom Ary had known before the World War II, and Madame Droze's participation in the resistance movement during the German occupation. Frances Stillman completes her diary by noting that she and Ary made an effort to see the art, the people, and the country from within their own environments. Microfilm roll 99, frames 1014-1230, and roll 100, frames 1-89.

ALINE SAARINEN (1914-1972)
Art critic, historian, New York, N.Y.

Correspondence among Saarinen, art historian Bernard Berenson, and his secretary, Nicky Mariano, 1953-1959 and undated (ca. 100 items). Berenson supplies biographical information about Isabella Stewart Gardner for a chapter on Gardner in Saarinen's book, *The Proud Possessors* (1958). Their letters chronicle the growth of an affectionate friendship and the exchange of intimate knowledge of museum curators, writers, and artists, including Chick Austin, Alfred and Daisy Barr, Saarinen's architect husband Eero, Peggy Guggenheim, Ezra Pound, James Rorimer, and Francis Henry Taylor. Saarinen's papers include notes on a 1953 visit to Berenson's home, I Tatti; her review of Berenson's "Essays in Appreciation"; and her tribute written on the occasion of his death. Also included is a draft of Saarinen's short story "The Triumph of Death," in which the characters represent the author and Berenson. Microfilm roll 2069, frames 506-797.

Photograph of Bernard Berenson wrapped in a shroud and lying on his death bed. Microfilm roll 2069, section 4.

ANNA WALINSKA (b. 1916?)
American artist, Italy

Two travel diaries kept in Italy, March-April 1955 (21 pp.) and April 12-May 1955 (36 pp.). In daily entries, Walinski describes the works and cathedrals that she sees, the cafés she visits, the beauty of the countryside, her visit with Randall Williams at the U.S. embassy, and her lunch date with Bulgarian sculptor Assew Perkov. Cities she visits include Arezzo, Assisi, Bologna, Florence, Perugia, Ravenna, Rome, and Venice. In Rome, she describes going to the Gallery of Modern Art and liking English artist Alan Davie's *Blue Triangle* (1953). Not microfilmed.

Letter from American artist Mona Sullivan, April 16, 1974. Sullivan describes her recent move to Rome and the adjustments to be made in language and culture. The letter is personal and sentimental, as she explains to Anna how important their friendship is to her. Not microfilmed.

DRAWING SOCIETY
New York, N.Y.

Issue of *Drawing* published by the Drawing Society, 1958 (67 pp.). The magazine has a section of 22 drawings by contemporary Italian artists and another section of 33 drawings by contemporary American artists. Each section is preceded by an introduction and a poem written by the editors: Daniel Brown, Bruce Duff Hooten, and David Johnson. They express their philosophy behind their decision to assemble drawings from different countries: "We do not believe that art begins or ends within national boundaries." Microfilm roll D 177, frames 252-286. Original privately owned.

ADDISON BURBANK (1898-1961)
American painter, writer, Italy

One sketchbook containing ca. 20 drawings of people, architecture, and marine scenes from Burbank's travels in southern Italy and Sicily, 1959; ca. 55 miscellaneous drawings possibly of Italian subjects. Microfilm roll 892, frames 401-498.

STANTON MACDONALD-WRIGHT (1890-1973)
American painter, Italy

Eighteen letters to his former student, painter Jan Stussy, 1959-1973. In 12 letters written during his trips to Florence and Lucca, Macdonald-Wright discusses his deteriorating health; visits to towns including Arezzo, Fiesole, Ravenna, San Gimignano, Siena, and Venice; and artists and works including Michelangelo and the church of San Vitale. MacDonald-Wright also writes 6 letters to Stussy in Rome, discussing Italian culture and mutual friend Bob Schneider, and offering encouragement for her work. Microfilm roll 2728, frames 4-360.

LOUIS BOUCHE (1896-1969)
American painter, Rome, Italy

Letter to Raphael Soyer, written while Bouché was at the American Academy in Rome, December 31, 1960. Bouché praises a catalog of Soyer's recent exhibition and Soyer's Skowhegan lecture. He writes of his favorite Italian masters--Piero della Francesca, Giotto, and Tiepolo--and he criticizes the "paint throwing" technique that has become popular in Europe. Microfilm roll N68-1, frame 74.

ELSIE DRIGGS (b. 1898)
Painter, New York, N.Y.

Typed letter to her, Maurice Sterne, and others from their friend S[?] describing his return to Anticoli-Corrado, Italy, 1960-1963 (5 pp.). He writes that the small town has not changed in the 20 years since they have lived there. Microfilm roll D 160, frames 220-224. Originals in the Elsie Driggs Papers.

BENJAMIN ROWLAND (1904-1972)
American art historian, collector, Cambridge, Mass., and Florence, Italy

Letters, 2 customs declarations, 1 postcard, and photographs of Italian and Roman sculptures and paintings Rowland purchased and sold while he worked as a collector at Harvard University's Fogg Art Museum, 1961-1966 (ca. 75 items). Also included is a letter asking Rowland if he would be available for the resident historian position at Villa I Tatti, October 30, 1964, and a letter from Mario Barsanti concerning the purchase of the Italian painting *Portrait of a Man in a Red Hat* by Dosso Dossi (undated). Microfilm roll 1079, frames 857-1087, 1184-1188.

NELSON SHANKS
Florence, Italy

Letter to Edward Fitzgerald, June 13, 1961. Shanks explains that he cannot afford even the small expense of belonging to a cooperative gallery and asks for "inactive" status. Not microfilmed.

FESTIVAL OF TWO WORLDS, SCULPTURE IN THE CITY
Spoleto, Italy

Letters (typescripts and originals), postcards, drawings, telegrams, and customs declarations for artwork, October 11, 1962-August 21, 1963 (ca. 120 items, some in Italian). Most correspondence concerns the exhibition "Sculpture in the City" which Giovanni Carandente, Italian art critic and museum director, coordinated. Herbert Ferber of New York, N.Y., asks Carandente if he knows of a place in Italy where he can make a large sculpture in sheet bronze and writes that he will bring a model of the sculpture to Italy. He also writes of travels in Italy and Paris to visit foundries. Carandente thanks him for the drawing and says he hopes Ferber will decide to cast his sculpture in Rome. Carandente writes Alexander Calder in Roxbury, Conn., and Indre et Loire, France, and asks Calder to make a large mobile for the exhibition to be placed like a triumphal arch over a road in Spoleto. Calder agrees to do the project, requests more details, and asks if he will be reimbursed for expenses. Calder later writes that he has decided to make a stabile *Teodelapio* instead of a mobile. After shipment of the model to Italsider, a workshop in Italy, Calder requests progress reports and repeatedly asks for photographs of prospective locations for the stabile and of the completed work. Letters concerning contract negotiations between Calder and the City of Spoleto outline how the city will care for the sculpture. Carandente also tells Calder that he has an idea for another exhibition at Spoleto, "New Forms in an Old City," and asks Calder if he would be interested in designing some bus stops for it. Carandente asks David Smith of Bolton Landing, N.Y., and Milan, Italy, to send his work to the Spoleto exhibition and thanks him for agreeing to participate. Smith writes that he has sent a sculpture to Italsider. Carandente writes to Boris Lurie in New York, N.Y., that he is planning to spend some time in the United States. Lurie writes that he is willing to work on details for the exhibition and that articles about his work are to be published in *ArtNews* and *Artforum*. Microfilm roll ITRO 1, frames 1-134. Originals in the Detroit Institute of Arts, Detroit, Mich.

ALAN ROBERT SOLOMON (1920-1973)
American art critic and historian, U.S. commissioner of the Biennale, Venice, Italy

Correspondence and papers, including 3 articles comparing American and Italian art, ca. 1963-1968; a guest book, 1964; business records, 1963-1964 and undated; and photographs, 1964 and undated; most of which pertain to his years in Venice as the U.S. commissioner of the Biennale. There is also correspondence pertaining to the preparations for the Biennale as well as letters congratulating Solomon on the success of the exhibit, November 7, 1963-October 31, 1964. Microfilm roll 3921, frames 320-900.

Business records, relating to expenditures for the Biennale and including purchase orders, receipts, and reimbursements, as well as an itemized expense ledger, ca. 1963-1964 and undated (21 pp.) Microfilm roll 3925, frames 1137, 1159, 1230-1244.

Papers, including a report (7 pp.) and a typescript (11 pp.) on the American artists' participation at the XXXII Biennale in Venice, June-October 1964, written while Solomon served as the U.S. commissioner who curated the American exhibition at the Biennale. He comments on the sponsorship of the American government as well as the generally negative reaction of European artists to Robert Rauschenberg's winning the First International Prize. Solomon describes the lack of exhibition space at the Biennale and explains the Americans' controversial decision to use the empty American consulate for additional exhibition space. In addition, there is a guest book from the United States pavilion at the XXXII Biennale as well as a list of artists who won prizes at various Biennales. Microfilm roll 3924, frames 7-24.

Edited draft of a manuscript for *L'Espresso* in English (12 pp.) and the completed article, "Mercenate Non Varca L'Oceano," in Italian (1 p.), August 1966. Solomon writes that he has "become conscious of some interesting contrasts between the ambient of art in Italy and America." He discusses various reasons for the increasing popularity of contemporary art in the United States, for which there is no parallel in Italy. Some of the reasons he lists relate to the predominantly private funding of American museums, tax laws that encourage donations to charitable institutions, and American businesses that underwrite cultural events. He encourages the opening of contemporary art centers in Milan and Rome as a preliminary step in increasing the importance of contemporary art in Italy. Microfilm roll 3924, frames 182-196.

An article titled "Italian Art of the Mid-Sixties" is included in an exhibition catalog by Solomon, 1968 (19 pp.). It indicates the directions of the younger, lesser-known Italian artists. He criticizes the increasing isolation of the United States as its own contemporary art came to dominate internationally. He goes on to discuss differences between Italian and American artists that affect their art, such as personality and religion; however, he states that the nationalities share a "sense of modernity." He includes a brief biography, in English and Italian, of each of the 12 artists in the exhibition. Microfilm roll 3924, frames 57-108.

Photographs, mostly undated, of the artists who participated in the Biennale and their works, including Jasper Johns, Kenneth Noland, Claes Oldenburg, and Robert Rauschenberg. Microfilm roll 3927, frames 476-1406.

ABRAM SCHLEMOWITZ (b. 1911)
American sculptor, Rome, Italy

Three letters, 1 photograph, and 3 financial papers relating to Schlemowitz's study in Rome, ca. 1965-1969. The photograph shows the artist surrounded by his work in his studio, 1969. The financial documents, all in Italian, pertain to his studio rent. Sculptor Bill [Roneveral?] writes from Corsica to Schlemowitz in Rome about the difficulties of creating sculpture in a primitive environment, November 18, 1968. David Khahn requests photographs of Schlemowitz's work for a book he is publishing, March 10, 1969; and Schlemowitz writes to the Guggenheim Foundation requesting a renewal of his fellowship for the upcoming year, November 4, 1968. Not microfilmed.

BARTLETT H. HAYES, JR. (b. 1904)
Director of the American Academy in Rome, Italy

Twelve letters relating to his association with the American Academy in Rome, 1965-1970. Included is a 4-pp. letter, October 21, 1965, to the director of the Academy,

Richard Kimball, describing his impressions of the Academy in 1965 and comparing it with the Academy in 1931-1932. Hayes suggests some changes and discusses, individually, the current fellows and their potential to be successful artists: Richard Ellis, Gregory Gillespie, Philip Grausman, Jack Henderson, William Ouelette, Charles Perry, Roger Ricco, Henry Rollings, Ray Saunders (from whom he bought 2 drawings for the Addison Gallery Collection), and Charles Wells. Hayes mentions 2 Italian artists, Aldo Casanova and Romas Vlesulas, to whom the Academy is renting facilities (frames 142-145). Kimball replies on December 14, 1965, describing his unexpected 12-day overseas journey on the *Raffaello* and giving Hayes more information about the Academy fellows Hayes met, including Casanova, Ellis, Gillespie, Grausman, Henderson, Ouellette, Perry, Ricco, Rollins, and Saunders. In a second letter, Hayes thanks Kimball for the information and informs him of the recent sale of Gillespie's *Strolling Nudes* to the Whitney Museum of American Art. James M. Walton thanks Hayes for his lecture in Rome and requests information about a painting by Allan D'Arcangelo titled *Full Moon*. In his response, Hayes encloses a slide of the painting. In addition there is a letter from Aldo Casanova, May 25, 1965, describing his work on his sculpture "a large Scarab in a rectangular composition." Included are the conditions and terms of employment. Microfilm roll 3932, frames 133-402.

GREGORIO PRESTOPINO (1907-1984)
American painter, New Jersey and Italy

Ca. 15 letters from the American Academy in Rome regarding his appointment as artist in residence for the academic year 1968-1969. Included are 2 letters from the director, Frank E. Brown, inviting Prestopino to be a painter in residence, and 4 from the Academy's secretary, Mary T. Williams, suggesting that he travel overseas aboard the *Michelangelo*, offering him a grant in honorarium, and informing him of the renewed fellows, Albert R. Lam III, Richard G. Kenworthy, and Kenneth R. Worley. Also included are 4 letters from Julian Levi, in which he wishes Prestopino a wonderful year in Italy and offers advice on Prestopino's poor heart condition, August-September 1968; 1 from Joseph Jay Deiss of the Academy, discussing living arrangements that will best accommodate Prestopino's heart condition; 2 letters of rejection for grants from the Ford Foundation and the National Council on the Arts; and 1 undated letter to Mary T. Williams, in which Prestopino discusses his transportation to Rome. Microfilm roll N68-88, frames 51-253. Originals privately owned.

WILLIAM T. WILEY (b. 1937)
American painter, Italy

Journal, written while in Italy with illustrations, poems, philosophical essays, and sketches, 1971 (35 pp.). Wiley mentions sending a painting to an exhibition and expresses his ideas on art: "I don't try to care about art as something to achieve--but as a concept for making known and sharing--information." Microfilm roll 910, frames 1-35. Restricted access. Use requires prior permission.

ALLAN OTHO SMITH (b. 1949)
Artist, Houston, Tex.

Eight journals-sketchbooks, containing his ideas on art, lists of instructions for understanding the human figure, and notes on line and balance as well as philosophical essays and poems, 1973-1979 (635 pp.). Smith offers a diagram of his studio and refers to artists Marcel Duchamp, Robert Rauschenberg, and Mark Rothko. Also included is an account of his travels in Italy, where he visited Padua, Rome, and Venice. He described his experience: "Europe is carving a procession of figures, places, and objects on the wooden box that is me." The drawings and sketches are in pencil and of animals, cars, the human figure, and machines. Microfilm roll 1655, frames 137-787. Originals privately owned.

WILLIAM CALFEE (b. 1909)
American sculptor, Italy

Illustrated travel diary of his trip to Rome, Florence, and Arezzo, May-August 1977 (unbound, 106 pp.). Calfee records his philosophical reflections and his observations of the people and places he encounters. Included are several pen-and-pencil sketches. Not microfilmed.

INDEX